arcus scratched his stubbled chin thoughtfully. "Oh…there are still a lot of issues being decided. Legislation has been passed to keep the water levels from being lowered further, but it isn't a real clear-cut victory. Mainly, it's important that the public remain informed…and aware."

"And that's where you come in." Green eyes stared at him intently, daring him to disagree.

"Now, Celia. Don't start.…"

"What's the big deal? It's what you do best, isn't it?"

"I won't be doing *any*thing if the magazine goes down. Come on, let's not argue.…"

"You said you like to fight with me." She gave him an impish grin.

"That's true." Marcus reached out and touched her cheek with gentle fingers. "But there's something I'd like to do more."

"Oh?" Celia's voice was little more than a breath. "There is?"

"There is." Marcus held her eyes firmly with his own. Celia's pulse quickened, and the sound of her pounding heart echoed in her ears as he drew near. Her eyes slipped to the hard line of his jaw, the crazy curve of his lips, the mischievous glint in his eyes.…

Palisades.
Pure Romance.

FICTION THAT FEATURES CREDIBLE CHARACTERS AND
ENTERTAINING PLOT LINES, WHILE CONTINUING TO UPHOLD
STRONG CHRISTIAN VALUES. FROM HIGH ADVENTURE
TO TENDER STORIES OF THE HEART, EACH PALISADES
ROMANCE IS AN UNDILUTED STORY OF LOVE,
FROM BEGINNING TO END!

A PALISADES CONTEMPORARY ROMANCE

SIERRA

SHARI MACDONALD

PALISADES

This is a work of fiction. The characters, incidents, and dialogues are products of the author's imagination and are not to be construed as real. Any resemblance to actual events or persons, living or dead, is entirely coincidental.

SIERRA
published by Palisades
a part of the Questar publishing family

© 1995 by Shari MacDonald
International Standard Book Number: 0-88070-726-7

Cover illustration by George Angelini
Cover designed by David Carlson
Edited by Gloria Kempton

Printed in the United States of America

For information:
QUESTAR PUBLISHERS, INC.
POST OFFICE BOX 1720
SISTERS, OREGON 97759

95 96 97 98 99 00 01 02 — 10 9 8 7 6 5 4 3 2 1

To my wonderful mom,
Jean Lynelle Burroughs MacDonald,
with love.

How incredible that one finite human body should contain
a heart as limitless as yours.
There is no greater evidence of God's love for me
than in the fact that I was born to you.

*"Oh, these vast, calm, measureless mountain days...
days in whose light everything seems equally divine, opening
a thousand windows to show us God."*

John Muir, *My First Summer in the Sierra*

One

✒

"No untroubled day has ever dawned for me."
Seneca

The sun sank low on the horizon, gracing purple-shadowed foothills with beams of pale spun-gold. One chipped, white diesel pump leaned awkwardly at the side of the highway, a long-abandoned witness to the years of intermittent traffic that had rushed through but rarely paused within the boundaries of Lundy proper.

Behind the wheel of her battered '69 Mustang, Celia yawned and stretched one slim, graceful arm, then the other. "Looks like this is it." She let up on the gas, reluctantly obeying the bright green sign ahead. Though the evening was young, the drive had taken its toll, and her mind held thoughts of little but bath and bed. "What do you say, Hank?" She glanced at the sad-eyed passenger beside her. "Shall we grab a bite before crashing at the new digs?"

At the sound of her voice, the chunky hound tore his eyes from the passing scenery and turned a loving gaze on his owner.

"Now, don't get any big ideas." Celia's voice was stern. "You're on probation, remember? I don't need a repeat of the Memphis chicken incident. But…a dog's got to eat. How about it? Do we need to break out the leash, or can you actually behave yourself?"

Hank blinked at her in adoration, then returned to his vigil at the window.

"Go ahead. Plead the Fifth. See if I care."

Celia wiggled her toes to relieve the cramps brought on by long hours of driving and ran her fingers through her dark, cropped curls. She sighed. The five-day trip from Atlanta had been exhausting. *But Paul would have loved it.* The image of a slim, tanned face and laughing eyes sprung unbidden into her mind. Celia shook her head as if to banish it. Memories were still vivid; it took effort to control them.

"Look!" The sight of a street sign ahead broke Celia's train of thought. "Northeast Hickory. I think that's where the office is located."

Hank obediently looked in the direction she pointed.

"You don't seem too excited. What's the matter? Don't you want to see home base?" Celia quickly turned at the narrow cross street, then fished a scrap of paper out of her purse and checked the address against the buildings they passed.

"Four-two-three…four-two-seven…A-*ha!* Four-two-nine. Bingo! This is it." She pointed to an attractive structure directly across the road, apparently the replica of an old general store. "The home office of *High Sierra* magazine." Celia pulled up in front of an empty ball field and parked behind a mud-spattered Land Cruiser, the only other vehicle in sight. "Let's get a better look. Come on! Give me two minutes, then I promise you dinner fit for a Doberman."

The hound *whoofed* in response and eagerly jumped out of the driver's-side door.

Celia walked across the street toward the office, her admiration growing with each step. It was clear that many of the buildings in Lundy were designed to capture the feel of the Old West. But none she'd seen in passing had appeared as authentic as this one. She climbed three wide stairs to an enormous wooden porch, then paused to examine its great log banisters and pine walls. The beams felt polished and splinterless under her hand, worn smooth from years of wear.

"My goodness! This place is *old*, Furball. I think it's the real thing just spruced up a bit here and there."

The main entrance was only a few feet from where Celia stood. But before she could step toward it, her attention was diverted by the sound of toenails clicking on hardwood as Hank trotted to the end of the porch and disappeared.

"Hey, Magellan," she called. "Wait up!"

Following after her pet, Celia discovered that the porch extended along the left side and around the back of the building. There, she found her hound sitting proudly on top of a weather-stained Adirondak chair, his nose raised high as he sniffed the air repeatedly in assessment of his surroundings.

Smiling at his obvious contentment, Celia turned to survey the view.

"Whew!" She let her breath out slowly. Along the horizon, granite cliffs jutted high against the sky. Frosted by a layer of pure snow, they appeared untouched, unspoiled; kindred spirits standing shoulder to shoulder against the intrusion of man.

"Hello, ladies," Celia whispered up at the powdered peaks. She stood at their feet, feeling small yet strangely significant.

After long days of highway noise and radio static, the magnitude of the silence triggered feelings of both shock and relief. Then a door slammed, followed by the close, familiar sound of clicking toenails.

"Stick close to Mom, Hank, " she called over her shoulder. "Okay? Hank?" She turned, but the dog was gone.

"Oh, for crying out loud...Hank?" Celia hurried toward the front of the building, her heart beating faster as a car engine roared to life.

"Hank! HANK!" She leaped down the front steps. Running toward the street, she spied the animal trotting cheerfully in the direction of the Land Cruiser. The driver had already backed up several feet and was now beginning to roll forward into the road.

"Stop! STOP, I SAID!" Celia bounded across both lanes and threw herself against the four-wheel-drive. The vehicle grazed her arm, knocking her off balance as it lurched to a halt.

"Oof!" Celia landed with a thud on something soft, her mind absently registering the sound of a smothered yelp. As she lay on the concrete trying to catch her breath, a tall, athletic-looking man with dark hair and wild eyes jumped out of the vehicle, leaving its door open behind him.

"Are you all right?" He rushed toward her. "I...."

Celia sat up and pointed at the man angrily, her green eyes flashing.

He stopped in his tracks.

"You! You almost killed Hank!" she accused breathlessly. "He was right in front of you, and you almost flattened him!" She sat up gingerly and immediately bent over the animal cowering at her side.

The man looked confused. "But I didn't see anyone…I don't understand how I..…" He peered around the front of the Land Cruiser. "I'm so sorry. Is he all right? Where…?"

Celia gave the tall stranger a look of disgust. "You can't see *anything,* can you? That explains a lot." She turned back to Hank, who wriggled cheerfully under her examination, the fright of the previous moment forgotten.

"What…the *dog?* You threw yourself in front of my truck for a dog? What kind of a crazy person are you? Do you have any idea what you just did? *You're* the one who could have been killed!"

Hank cried out softly as Celia ran her fingers along his tail. "Sorry, bud," she mumbled consolingly. She glared at the man who loomed over her.

"Very nice. First you try to kill my dog. Then you lecture me about living a long life. I'd love to hear more of your valuable advice, but I'm sure you're pretty busy, beating up little old ladies, robbing lemonade stands…or whatever it is you do that's so important you had to rush off without even *looking where you were going.*" Celia scooped Hank up in her arms and stood, drawing herself up to her full five feet four inches of height. She barely reached the man's chin.

The stranger folded his arms and returned her angry look. "Not only are you insane," he said calmly, "you also seem to be hallucinating. If you think I'm the one in the wrong here, I suggest you have your head examined. I may have hit you harder than we realized."

Celia's eyes narrowed to mere slits. "There is nothing wrong with me that your absence won't cure," she said icily. She gave the man one more glare, turned on her heel, and marched back to her car. Upon reaching it, she groaned, realizing the difficulty she would have getting Hank back inside the vehicle. But before she could make a move, the man was beside her, his hand on the passenger door.

"Wait. Look, that came out all wrong. Can we start again here? I really am sorry. But he...Frank, you said? He looks just fine to me. You're the one I'm worried about. For a minute there, I thought...."

Celia lay the dog gently on the bucket seat and muttered through clenched teeth, "We'll both be fine. If you'll excuse me." She slammed the car door, stalked to the driver's side and climbed in, then sped away without another glance.

The man shook his head and stared as the Mustang became a black speck in the distance. *There goes the most aggravating and beautiful woman I've ever met in my life.*

Two

> *"…I was a stranger, and you invited me in.…"*
> Matthew 25:35, The Holy Bible

Celia located a vet's office simply by pulling over at a nearby corner and asking directions of a local teenager, whose eyes widened at the sight of the beautiful stranger.

"Two blocks down, and left on Sonora. Want me to show you?" the sun-browned boy suggested hopefully.

Celia smiled graciously, ignoring his innocent flirtation. "Thanks, but I've got it."

She inched back onto the road and encouraged her passenger, "See, Hank? We're almost there. We'll get you fixed up in no time."

Hank gave Celia a droopy-eyed stare, as if he'd just been rudely awakened from a deep and much-needed slumber.

"All right," she said. "Indulge me. You may *think* you're fine, but I'll feel better once you've been looked at by a doctor. Humor your mother."

The white building was small but easy to spot. A large beautifully carved wooden sign stood by the roadside, proclaiming to passing traffic: VALERIE JAMES, D.V.M. • 24-HOUR CARE.

"Well, *that's* a blessing!" Celia recalled the night in Atlanta when the hound had cheerfully swallowed a Pepsi cap. Three hours and one extremely unpleasant examination later, Celia received a vet bill that made her gasp, as well as a list of referrals that Hank's regular doctor suggested would be "closer to your home—more convenient in cases of emergency, I'm sure."

"Let's just hope Valerie James doesn't come to curse the day you were born."

The waiting room was empty, but from beyond the back wall came the faint chorus of yelping dogs and wailing felines. Stuck to the reception counter was a curled, faded note, bearing the scribbled message: "Ring Bell for Service." Celia pushed an ancient-looking metal button she assumed must sound in the kennels, then settled into an orange vinyl armchair that squeaked rudely beneath her. Hank, held firmly in Celia's arms, tried to wriggle free.

"I know, I know. But it's not what you think. Sure, it *smells* like the place where you get your shots. But that's not our mission today. Honest." From the next room, the sound of barking grew markedly louder.

Hank gave her a baleful stare.

"I *swear!* Have I ever lied to you? I mean…you know, when it really counts?"

After several minutes, the door to the back room swung open and a tall, slender woman in a white lab coat emerged. Her sun-lightened hair was gathered in a loose ponytail, revealing classic features and flawless, alabaster skin. Bright hazel eyes peered at Celia from under a fringe of golden bangs.

"Hi! Valerie James," she announced brightly. "Sorry you had to wait. It's feeding time." Celia stood and followed the woman down a narrow corridor to a small, well-scrubbed room that smelled of disinfectant and animal dander. "All right." The woman placed her hands on her hips and asked cheerfully, "What have we got here?"

Lifting Hank onto the examination table, Celia explained, "Let me introduce Hank, klutz king of the canine world. He just had a near-fatal encounter with a Land Cruiser."

"Where was he hit?" The doctor softly prodded the animal's ribs, his legs, his hips while Hank slipped and slid around on the table trying to jump off.

"It's his tail, I think." Celia paced nervously. "He sort of…that is, he wasn't actually *hit* so much as…well, if that jerk had just been watching where he was going!"

Valerie whispered soothingly to Hank while her gentle fingers found his area of injury. He whined softly but finally remained still under her touch. The veterinarian glanced up at Celia in surprise. "This looks *incredibly* minor to have been caused by a vehicle. I can't imagine…."

Celia cleared her throat. "It, uh, didn't actually run *over* his tail. It's more like it made me—um…."

Valerie raised her eyebrows curiously.

"I sort of, uh…landed on him."

The blonde grinned at Celia's obvious embarrassment. "And would you, by chance, happen to be the klutz queen of the *human* world?"

Celia gave her a wan smile. "That would be me. Life with Hank must be taking its toll." She watched as Valerie wrapped the animal's tail in soft, white gauze, then a heavy tape.

"There," the woman said. "Hank will be fine. His tail isn't

too badly bruised. He hasn't lost any feeling at the tip. This will just help protect it while he heals."

Hank bestowed upon the women a look of eternal patience.

"Look at him," Celia remarked. "He's got 'I told you so' written all over his face. He didn't even want to come."

Valerie tried to conceal her amusement. "You and Hank seem to understand each other very well."

Celia nodded sheepishly and stroked the hound's back. "Yeah, I suppose we do. I forget how silly we—I—must look to a stranger. I'm really not a wacko. It's just that he's the only family I've got." She looked fondly at the animal, who was wriggling happily now under her fingers. "Isn't that right, Hairball?"

Celia turned back to the blonde. "I got him a few years back, at the pound. I just picked him up one day to keep me company on my road trip. Now, which one was it?" Her voice trailed off. "I think I was going to Charlotte that time...or was it Nashville? Anyway, I just did it on a whim; now he's my best friend. Sometimes I forget that he doesn't get everything I say. He really seems to understand and, you know, sometimes I could swear I know what he's thinking, too."

Valerie nodded. "At times, you probably do."

Celia stopped scratching Hank's ears and grinned. "Wow. Listen to me go off! And you got all that from a perfect stranger. Sorry. Allow me to introduce myself. Celia Randall—human klutz queen and nut case extraordinaire."

"Hello, Celia Randall." The blonde nodded agreeably. "Valerie James—mender of canine klutzes and nut case sympathizers."

The two women smiled at each other companionably.

"Well, I'm glad I got to meet you while you were in town. I assume you're headed somewhere tonight? Obviously, you aren't a local, or I'd know you and Hank by now—"

"You don't know the half of it," Celia muttered.

Valerie grinned. "How far are you driving tonight?"

"Actually, this is it," Celia admitted. "Destination: Lundy. Hank and I have a little rental over on Whitney. Haven't even seen it yet."

"I don't know what you had planned, but if you'd like a cup of hot tea before you head out, you're more than welcome," Valerie offered.

Celia hesitated. "Actually, we've been on the road all day, and Hank and I have both *got* to get some food."

"Well, I'm no Julia Child, but if you'd like to join me for a bowl of hot soup, I'd love to have the company. My place is right next door. And something tells me there's *something* around here Hank could eat."

Celia considered the friendly face before her and the rumbling of her stomach. "Weeell, if you're sure it's no trouble...."

"Not a bit. Let me just grab some kibble and lock up." Valerie disappeared into the hall.

Celia looked down at the melancholy animal beside her. "I know, I know—hospital food. Sorry." She leaned down and whispered conspiratorially, "We'll order you a pizza later."

Three

"The more I see of men, the better I like dogs."
Madame Roland

S o, what brings you to Lundy?" The warm, daffodil-colored kitchen was filled with the sweet smell of simmering tomato soup. Valerie stood at the butcher's block slicing generous crusts of wheat bread and thick wedges of cheddar to grill. At her feet, Hank resigned himself to nuzzling a bowl filled with equal portions of high-quality canned dog food and dry nuggets. ("It's better for him than people food," the veterinarian had insisted.)

"My work." Celia sat at the bay window, gazing out at the clear, brilliant night sky. She blew softly into the ceramic mug in her hands, savoring the aroma of blackberry and herbs. After giving it several moments to cool, she took a long sip of the tangy tea, delighting in the relief to her parched tongue.

"I'm a freelance photographer," she continued. "I've lived in Atlanta for the past five or six years, but it's more of a home base than anything else. I travel quite a bit; more and more in the past year. I'm here now on a short-term assignment for *High Sierra* magazine. After that, well…who knows? I've been thinking about trying someplace new. I may even try basing myself on the West Coast for awhile."

Valerie looked surprised. "That's a switch. Why would you want to do that?"

"Oh…no reason in particular," Celia hedged. "I'd just like the change of pace, I guess. Maybe a little adventure."

"A little romance?"

"Huh?" Celia said in a startled tone.

"You know. There's just something romantic about a young woman taking off on her own, traveling to someplace unknown. Anything could happen!" She registered Celia's blank stare. "What? Oh, come on. You're telling me you never think about it? The thought never crossed your mind?"

"What thought? Romance?"

"Sure. What might happen. *Who you might meet.*" Valerie looked delighted. "I wish I had the guts to try it." She paused for a moment. "Actually, I think I do have the guts. Just not the desire. I'm awfully happy the way things are. My roots are here…the folks aren't too far away. But what about you? It must be hard coming here all alone. What about friends, family? You were serious when you said you don't have anyone?"

"I was an only child. My father died when I was seventeen; my mom when I was twenty-one." Celia's voice was matter-of-fact. "After college, I went to an art school in Atlanta for a year and just never left." Her gaze drifted toward the window. "I still have a lot of friends in the South. But most of them are married by now. You probably know the drill. They start to have kids…you begin to feel like a fifth wheel." She shrugged. "There just isn't anyone who needs me terribly anymore. No one I couldn't leave." Her voice lowered to little more than a whisper. "No one who couldn't leave me."

At that moment, Hank clumsily stepped one foot into his

bowl of water, spilling its contents onto the linoleum floor.

"Okay, there's one guy who *definitely* needs me." Celia got to her feet and moved to clean up the mess. She looked lovingly at Hank, who had the decency to appear slightly embarrassed. "Sorry about that, Val."

"Not a problem. Paper towels are right behind you. And dinner's just about ready."

Minutes later, the two women were settled at the claw-foot dining table with a tureen of soup and a plateful of enormous sandwiches between them. Celia eyed them appreciatively. Back home, she rarely ever cooked; she found it hard to make the effort for just one person. Her eyes surveyed the cozy room. After days of travel and stark hotel rooms, Valerie's home was a feast to her eyes. She sighed and felt herself begin to relax within the comforting warmth. This must be part of the much-touted joy that came with small-town living.

"What about you? How'd you end up out here, in the middle of nowhere?" Celia made a sweeping gesture with her arm, as if to implicate the entire community.

"Oh, I'm a local girl. My parents still live in Placerville, where I grew up. I went away to school, like you did…lived in Phoenix for awhile. But I always felt a connection with the Gold Country. In the city, I could still smell the scent of pine and feel the dust and granite beneath my feet. I'd hear the wind whispering in the treetops, and I'd tell myself it was the Sierra calling me home." Valerie's cheeks turned slightly rosy. "I know. Weird, huh? But home I came. And I've never regretted it. I saved up my money and bought the building that's now my office. I'm renting this house, but I hope to own it some day, too. I enjoy being right next door to my work; I like being here for people."

"Small-town vet, huh? Just like in the books."

Valerie grinned. "You got it. And the movies. I saw *Dr. Doolittle* when I was just a little rug rat. I'd wander all over the house pretending I was on a journey to find the 'Great Pink Sea Snail.' Must have driven my mom crazy. When I got a little older, I read *All Creatures Great and Small*, and the other James Herriott books. I guess I never fully recovered."

Celia reflected on her own work: capturing brilliant color combinations, graceful shapes, miracles of nature. She contrasted that image with another one of spending days in Valerie's cramped office.

"I don't know," she said doubtfully. "It seems like a lot of work."

"Oh, but I love it. I've always adored animals. There's something about them that's so…vulnerable. They even make *me* feel vulnerable." Valerie looked thoughtful. "It's like…well, take the news, for example. Day after day after day there's so much violence against humanity committed *by* humanity. Ugh. It's easy to get hardened about people, I think. At least it is for me. But then, I sometimes wonder if that's unavoidable?" Valerie's thin, blonde eyebrows pinched together as she seemed to consider the moral dilemma. "I mean, if we were to truly anguish about all the horror in the world, we'd be crushed under the weight of the emotions, wouldn't we? So we build up these walls of indifference. But—" A small smile tugged at her rosy lips. "When I'm with the animals, somehow those walls come down for me. Each animal I treat reminds me of how interdependent we all are— how great is our need for compassion and mercy. I remember how precious life is, how fragile. When I was a child, my mother used to tell me: 'Not one sparrow falls to the ground without our

Father's knowledge.' I guess I just always wanted to be in a position to care for those sparrows."

Celia nodded. "When I was a kid, the boys down the street used to conduct these evil experiments on bugs, pulling off their wings, sticking them under a magnifying glass. Stuff like that. But not me. Nooo. Whenever I'd see an ant or a spider indoors, I'd have to rescue it and take it back outside. I still do that sometimes," she admitted. "Isn't that bizarre? I know it would be easier to squash them...and I could. I'm not a fanatic. It just seems to me that when given an equal choice, it's nobler to choose mercy."

Valerie furrowed her eyebrows, feigning concern. "You really *are* a nut case extraordinaire."

"Hmph. Takes one to know one," Celia countered cheerfully.

"So tell me more about this assignment over at *High Sierra*, O Crazy One." Valerie sunk her teeth into a mouthful of bread and cheese.

"Well, I don't know a whole lot about it myself yet. Apparently, some local artist saw some of my pieces at a show in Martha's Vineyard and told the editor of *High Sierra*, Marcus Stratton, that he liked my work. I got a call from Stratton's secretary three weeks ago. The photographer they planned on had a scheduling conflict. I sort of had the itch to get out of Atlanta anyway, so I jumped at the chance. We never really talked about specifics. It's something for their tenth anniversary issue."

"Ten years. That's incredible. That man's really made a go of it."

"What do you mean, 'go of it'?"

"Marcus started the magazine just over ten years ago, from a small room in his grandfather's cabin. When it finally got too big, a few years back, he moved into the old general store and has

26

run it from there, on a shoestring, ever since. Financially it's been hard, I think, though he never complains. Still—the magazine's won several awards and received critical acclaim, so that's something. I heard last year that it's finally beginning to turn a little bit of a profit. I'm glad for him."

"So you know Stratton?"

"We go to the same church. It's a small town. You can't help but know almost everyone. But we got to know each other a little better about a year or so ago when he brought in a stray German shepherd. He definitely made a lasting impression. That man could charm the socks right off the President's cat."

"Sounds cocky."

"Oh, not a bit! He's just, well...."

"Just what?"

"I suppose *captivating* would be the word. The women around here simply drool over him."

Celia felt uncomfortable. "Why doesn't he just pick one and get it over with?"

"Rumor has it he couldn't care less. I'm telling you, that magazine is his baby. He makes his appearances at local charity events, and so on. But beyond that, the man just isn't a social animal."

"No doubt, he's broken some poor girl's heart. Probably two or *three* girls." Celia felt herself becoming increasingly agitated.

"What? Where did you get th—"

"He probably just doesn't want to commit," she said, almost angrily.

"But that's not what I sa—"

"Well, he doesn't have a thing to worry about with me. I'm

going to go in tomorrow, get my assignment, and then *Adios, amigo*. I'm hitting the Muir Trail."

"I see." The blonde shifted awkwardly.

"Sorry." Celia sensed the other woman's discomfort and ceased her ranting. "I shouldn't have spouted off like that."

"Don't worry about it. You're tired, you've had a terrible day. You probably just need to go home and get some rest." She took the soup bowls from Celia's hands. "I can get this. You're welcome to stay as long as you like, but—"

"—but I know a certain basset hound who'd like nothing better than to find our new place, curl up on the bed, and dream about sausage and mushrooms with extra cheese."

"Ugh." The veterinarian covered her ears and gave a mock shudder. "I don't want to know."

Smiling, Celia stood and gathered her things. "Thanks for everything. You've been an angel."

"Anytime." Valerie set the bowls on the cream-colored tile counter and led Celia to the door. "Now, good luck tomorrow. And take it easy on Marcus. Men aren't all princes, but they're not all ogres, either. I think you'll find this one is a pretty decent guy."

Celia was unconvinced.

"Besides, he's your *boss*. Play nice."

"All right, all right. I get the point. Thanks." Celia's cheeks dimpled and her smile reached her deep green eyes. "I owe you one. How 'bout lunch next week?"

"You got it. Give me a call. I'm in the book, under 'D.' For 'Doolittle.'" She retreated into the house, whistling merrily, "If I Could Talk to the Animals."

Celia walked to her Mustang while Hank trotted happily at her side. Her decision to come to Lundy was looking better and wiser all the time.

Four

"*Sigh no more, ladies, sign no more, Men were deceivers, ever.*"
William Shakespeare, *Much Ado About Nothing*

D awn arrived bright and hopeful, painting the canvas sky with streaks of fuchsia and gold. Flecks of dust danced in the pale beams of light that shone through the window, awakening Celia from her heavy slumber.

"Augh!" One glance at the glowing, crimson numbers confirmed her worst fears. "Can you believe it? Day One, and I'm already late."

After a quick shower, Celia drew a heavy brush through her thick curls and reached into her overnight bag. Pulling out a slightly wrinkled tricot knit shirt and a crinkled gauze skirt, she muttered to the sleepy lump at the foot of her four-poster, "Don't worry. It's the latest style. *Seriously.* They'll think I'm chic."

Hopping from one foot to the other, Celia slipped battered leather sandals over toes in desperate need of fresh polish. As she rushed through the kitchen, she scalded her tongue on her morning coffee and half-choked on a stale blueberry bagel left over from her road trip. Wiping away tears triggered by the bagel, she scrambled around the house looking for her wayward keys.

"Grace under pressure. I cannot *believe* I'm like this."

After nearly ten minutes of hunting, Celia finally found the object of her search under a pile of discarded clothes. By this time, however, she was so far out of sorts, the discovery only made her grumble further.

"Great. I could have *walked* there and been back by now." Celia picked the lazy hound dog off her bed and carried him through the cozy living room, maneuvering around several threadbare easy chairs and bookcases filled with battered dime-store paperbacks. After planting a light kiss on the top of the animal's head, she placed him gently outside the back door. Hank gave her a sorrowful backward glance, then wandered reluctantly into the roomy fenced yard.

"Commune with nature for a while," she called after him. "I'm going to get our marching orders. Be back as soon as I can."

She glanced at her watch and groaned. Eight-thirty-five.

"I'm dead."

As Celia pulled up in front of the office building, she glanced into her rearview mirror and glared accusingly at her reflection.

"Phooey!" Mourning the fact that she wore no makeup other than a neutral eye shadow and earth-toned lipstick, she consoled herself, "Well, they didn't hire me for my looks." Taking a deep breath, she climbed out of the car, pointlessly smoothed her wrinkled skirt, and walked through the front door.

Rather than the bustling office atmosphere she expected, Celia found herself in a sea of dusty oak desks swimming under loose papers, stacks of dog-eared magazines, and piles of yellowed newspaper clippings. Behind one table sat a stout older woman with bright black eyes and even blacker hair, which had been thoroughly teased in an apparent attempt at a beehive.

"May I help you?" the woman offered.

"Yes, thanks. I'm Celia Randall. I have an appointment with Mr. Stratton."

"Of course." The beehive woman nodded. "We were expecting you. I'm Eva Bollerman, Mr. Stratton's assistant."

"Oh, Eva! You're the miracle worker I spoke with on the phone. Thanks for finding me the house. It's perfect."

The secretary beamed. "With so many vacation rentals coming up, it wasn't too hard to find you a week-by-week lease. Even furnished." The look on her face reminded Celia of Hank on the morning she'd introduced him to the joy of toaster waffles. "How are you settling in?"

"Well, all right so far. Unfortunately, I messed up my alarm and sort of overslept," Celia admitted nervously. "I was supposed to be here at eight-thirty."

The woman blinked at her.

"Uh...I'm late."

"Oh!" This statement threw the woman into action. "Of course. Just a moment." Eva dialed the phone and spoke in her most professional tone. "Mr. Stratton, Miss Randall is here." She smiled proudly at Celia, then glanced away and reverted to her normal speaking voice. "What, Marcus? Where? Yes, of course. All right." She turned to her visitor, looking slightly confused.

"He said to go on back...first office on your right."

"Thank you." Celia took a deep breath and started down the hall. She already felt too self-conscious and Eva's reaction to the phone conversation hadn't helped to alleviate her fears.

As she walked through the door, a slim blonde man with a golden tan and youthful appearance turned from a sketch-covered drawing board and moved to take her hand.

"Miss Randall." Gray eyes twinkled as he greeted her.

"Hello, Mr. Stratton. I'm *so* sorry I'm late. You just wouldn't believe the last two days I've had."

"Trouble?" He appeared sympathetic.

"The worst. But that's no excuse. Please do forgive me. I assure you, this flakiness is in no way a reflection on my competence as a photographer. I promise you'll be pleased with my work on this project."

"Don't give the matter a second thought. To tell you the truth—" The man turned his attention to a pile of messages laying on a credenza. "—I've had my hands full with a problem of my own. My car was totaled yesterday by a hit-and-run driver."

"That's terrible!"

"Isn't it? The police think there's a good chance of finding him, though. There were witnesses. This is a small town, with only one highway running through it. It's not like anyone can hide around here. And, after all, how many Land Cruisers can there possibly be in the area? I mean—"

Celia sucked in her breath. "Did you say *Land Cruiser?* Not a silver one, surely...."

"Why, yes. How did you guess?"

"This is incredible...you won't believe it. Just yesterday, that same creep nearly ran over me and my dog!"

"You're joking!" A tiny smirk tugged at the corner of the man's mouth.

"No, really! It was right outside this office, in fact. I don't think he was drunk or anything, but he certainly was an idiot!" Her voice was thick with passion. "I think he must have been legally blind; the guy definitely had *no* business being on the road. Oh, I hope you get him! It's just what that smart aleck deserves," she said with great relish. She stepped over to the window, which offered a northern view. "I don't know if you can see out front...oh, yes, you can. Right up there...I had just come around the other side of the building—" Celia stopped abruptly, spying a vehicle parked directly beneath them. "You know, you're right." She stiffened. "How many silver Land Cruisers can there possibly be around here?"

"How many indeed?" an amused voice questioned behind her.

Celia whirled around to find a tall, familiar-looking man propped against the door jamb.

"So...we meet again. How's Frank?"

Five

✤

"Be good, sweet maid, and let who will be clever.…"
Charles Kingsley

You've *got* to be kidding!" "I thought that had to be you yesterday." The handsome stranger folded well-defined arms across his chest and smirked. A lock of stray hair fell across deep blue eyes, and an expensive-looking tie hung loose around the buttoned-down collar of his denim shirt. "We were expecting Celia Randall on Monday, and Eva told me you had a dog. Who else would be snooping around the office like that—"

"*Snooping!* Of all the nerve—"

"Okay, poking. Digging. Prodding. Spying. Take your pick. The point is, no one else would have any business being here." He shrugged. "Not that you did either, *technically*, since you really weren't expected until Monday."

Celia strode across the room and positioned herself between the two men, standing with her back to the executive at the art table. "Okay. Ha-ha," she ground out in a low voice. "You've had your joke. Now if you'll *excuse* me, I'd like to finish my business with Mr. Stratton."

"Oh, of course. How silly of me," the stranger whispered. "Very sensible of you." Her Nemesis turned to the blonde and spoke in a loud voice. "I guess you can go, Rob. Fun's over."

"Sure thing, Marcus." The man grinned at Celia apologetically and moved to stand beside his coworker. She turned, aghast, from one to the other as realization dawned on her.

"*Oooh,* please tell me this is a bad dream," she moaned.

The real Mr. Stratton, her boss, the one she'd called a creep and an idiot two short minutes ago, shook his head as if expressing deep regret. "Sorry. I'd love to, but there's no time for chitchat. I'm giving a lecture this morning on twentieth-century torture techniques; I'm scheduled to evict a blind woman from her home at lunch time—" He ticked the tasks off on his fingers. "—I've got to huff and puff and blow a house down later this afternoon; and then I'm having a little get-together tonight with some of the other trolls."

"This has got to be sexual harassment or something," Celia protested weakly.

"Not at all. It was the perfect set-up." Stratton crossed the room and sat on the windowsill, looking thoroughly pleased with himself. "You walked right into our trap. We'd have tortured anybody under the circumstances. Isn't that right, Rob?" He turned casually to his partner in mischief.

"Yeah, that's pretty much true. We're just giving you a hard time," the blonde offered, as if that were all the explanation needed. He grinned and gave Celia a jaunty salute. "Rob Simmons, art director. I'll be working with you on your piece."

Celia stared at him blankly.

Rob's face fell. He ducked his head and shifted his weight from one foot to the other. "Or, uh…whatever. Nice to meet you." With one final guilty glance at Marcus, the designer made his escape.

The tiny brunette gave a small sigh and watched Rob go. Then she pivoted on her heel and glared at her tormentor. "I don't know whether to die of embarrassment or ream you! Are you going to have me escorted out under armed guard, or shall I just show myself to the door?"

"Don't be silly." Marcus's tone became noticeably more gentle. "It was never my intent to upset you. To humble you...without a doubt. To embarrass you...okay, maybe a little. You seemed so sure I was an ogre, I couldn't resist the temptation to prove you right. But you showed fire yesterday, real spunk. I felt sure you could take a joke. I never would have kidded around with you if I didn't." He paused. "I wasn't wrong, was I? You *can* take a joke?"

"Of *course* I can take a joke," Celia conceded grudgingly.

"Well, then! Great! You should feel honored. Rob and I do this to each other all the time. Now you're like one of the family."

"Lucky me," Celia muttered under her breath.

"What's that?"

"I said, 'Oh, that's just great.' Really. Thanks."

Marcus looked pleased. "Of course you did. Well, now that we've, ah...broken the ice, why don't we head back to my office and get started?"

Celia was relieved. "I thought you'd never ask."

"I think you'll find this one is a pretty decent guy." Oh, Valerie girl, did you ever miss the mark on this one.

Celia, trying to salvage what little dignity she had left, followed Marcus past the kitchenette to a second office.

"This is an extraordinary town. Wonderfully picturesque. I

37

feel like I'm really in the Old West." *Perfect. How banal can you get? This should take things back to the proper shallow level.*

"That's because you are." Marcus removed a stack of file folders from an oak broker's chair and nodded hospitably. "Please. Have a seat."

Celia did as she was directed and glanced out the window, trying hard to avoid eye contact. "A friend of mine mentioned the Gold Country. So I suppose we're near some historical mines?" She held her body tensely, and she knew her voice must sound strained.

Marcus appeared not to notice. "Actually, we're just down the road from Bodie, once one of the most profitable districts of its time. Over a hundred million dollars in gold was extracted from this area between 1859 and 1880." Celia glanced over, feigning interest, but her mind had already tuned him out. *Who does this guy think he is? Tour guide at Frontierland?*

But he continued, oblivious to her disdain. "The town's pretty famous. You may have heard of it. Ever hear of 'The Bad Man from Bodie'? Besides being incredibly prosperous, the place was notorious for drawing rotten, no-account men."

"Must be something in the water," Celia mumbled under her breath.

"What was that?"

"I, uh…was just wondering if I could get a glass of water?" Her look was one of wide-eyed innocence. "A-*hem*. Sorry. Mouth's dry."

An expression of amusement spread across the editor's face. "Of course." He inclined his head graciously.

Celia rolled her eyes at his retreating back, then took advantage of the opportunity to examine her surroundings. Directly in front of her, almost touching her knees, was an enormous, deep-grained oak desk she imagined old enough to be an antique but not likely to be of value; the sides and surface revealed heavy gouges, as if a restless schoolchild had dug into them with a pocket knife.

On top of the desk sat a personal computer of such large proportions that she assumed it had to be outdated. Against the machine were stacked Prentice Hall's *Handbook for Writers*, a student's pocket dictionary, a faded yellow *Roget's Thesaurus*, and a well-thumbed copy of Strunk & White's *Elements of Style*.

Darkly stained pine bookcases lined the walls; shelves were covered with the same hodge-podge mess that cluttered the building's greeting area. Behind the desk was a large unshuttered window, an open mouth calling silently to the mountains.

"I DROVE THROUGH SOME PRETTY DESOLATE COUNTRY ON MY WAY TO TOWN," Celia called after Marcus. "BUT HERE IT'S SO—Oh! Sorry." She jumped at finding him standing directly over her. Deep azure eyes studied her intently. "Here…here it's so fresh and green. Almost like, uh…paradise."

Marcus appeared poised to say something of great importance. But after a slight pause, he handed her a tumbler of water and moved away abruptly. "A lot of the foothills region is like that. It's not the most fertile country in the world, but a number of rivers and springs flow down from the peaks, cutting through on their way to the valley. Not too far from here, the land looks almost like a moonscape. But at this elevation, you'll find a variety of grasses—green and gold—bright wild mustard, brilliant California poppies…." His voice trailed off as he gazed out at the yawning window. "There's no place like it, anywhere."

Celia stared at him. The wonder in his voice sounded

genuine. *He almost sounded like a real person.*

"Well, shall we talk about the job?" Celia's manner was suddenly brisk. "During college I spent one full summer hiking the Pacific Rim, so I've had enough experience in the wilderness to handle the job, I think. I'm sure I won't have any trouble. Now, I don't know if you've got anything specific planned, but I've heard a lot about the Mono and Muir Trails, and I thought maybe I could start on one of those. If you could just get me a couple of trail maps and mark the spots you want me to—"

"Whoa! Slow down there." Marcus looked less than enthusiastic about her proposal. "Before you pack up your mule and head for the hills, I do think we'd better talk a little bit about the specifics of this assignment."

"Certainly." Celia eyed him nervously. "What exactly did you have in mind?"

Marcus rubbed his temples restlessly. "Didn't Eva give you any details at all?"

"Not really. She mentioned you were in a spot, and you needed someone right away. She said this was an anniversary issue, so I assume the piece is especially important. Is that what you're asking?" When Marcus did not respond, she went on, "The timing was perfect for me. It seemed like an act of providence." Celia felt increasingly nervous. "I offered to send my portfolio, but she said it wasn't necessary—"

"No, of course not. Not at **all**. Dave Lassen gave your work his stamp of approval, and that's all I need. No, I'm referring to the details of this *specific* assignment. Didn't you ask Eva what you'd be shooting?"

"Nooo," Celia responded slowly. "Let me take a wild guess— The Sierra?"

"Close, but no cigar. Actually, this assignment is the photo shoot for our cover article: 'Top Five Inns of the Sierra Nevada.'"

Celia cocked her head and leaned forward in her chair. "Excuse me?"

"You know…a nice, schmaltzy piece about the crisp, clean air; the crystal streams; the best places to 'get away from it all'…blah, blah, blah." His voice held a trace of cynicism.

"But I…I just assumed.…" Celia chose her words carefully. "As an artist, I focus on the sort of work that showcases my talents professionally—"

"I realize that." Marcus nodded patiently. "But, like most freelance artists, I gather you accept 'lesser' projects as well, to help pay the bills?"

"Well, yes. But you must realize you're talking about an entirely different type of photography than what I normally do. You'll need indoor photos, still shots—"

"You can do it, can't you?"

Celia bristled. "Well, of course I can do it! It's just that it's not my specialty—"

"You have everything you need?"

She nodded. "I brought all my equipment. That's not the problem. It's simply that in this case…like I said, I just assumed—"

Stratton stepped away from the window and stood before Celia, his expression strained. "Miss Randall, I am sorrier about this situation than you will ever know…for more reasons than one. Eva is a wonderful woman. However, she's not always as thorough as I might like. I should have spoken with you about the job myself. I truly wish I had a more substantial piece to offer you, but unfortunately, at this time I don't."

"Surely, with your tenth anniversary issue—"

"No." Marcus's voice was firm, almost harsh. A look of frustration passed over his face. Then, as quickly as it had appeared, it was gone. "It would be an honor and a pleasure to work with you on this piece." His tone softened. "We stand by our bid for your services. In fact, considering all that I've put you through, I'd like to offer you a modest bonus. Uh…'modest' being the operative word here." Blue eyes, once stormy, now twinkled. Marcus took Celia's small, white hand between his large, tanned ones and squeezed it warmly. She shuddered as a tiny thrill ran up her spine. "Unfortunately, that's all I have to offer. I would be *terribly* disappointed if you declined." His eyes seemed to hold more than his words revealed. "But I also sympathize with your position."

Celia sat in silence, considering her options. *I can always go back to Atlanta. But it's as if Paul is still there.…* "No. I'll stay," she promised resolutely. "I said I'd do the job and I'm going to do the job. It's a disappointment, of course. But I'll manage."

Marcus's face slipped into an expression of professional satisfaction. "I'm glad to hear it. Very glad, indeed." He stepped back and lifted a battered manila folder from his desk. "Here's a list of the inns I'd like you to shoot and an outline of their distinctive features, as well as maps and details about their locations. All are within a 25-mile radius—easy driving distance. Start wherever you'd like." He lifted a large pile off one burgeoning bookshelf.

"Let me carry this stack of back issues out to your car for you. You can browse through them at your leisure. They'll give you an idea of what *High Sierra* is all about. At least, what it's *supposed* to be about," he amended wryly. "Can you start tomorrow?"

"Of course."

Celia followed Marcus into the hallway, where he bestowed upon her one last gracious smile. "Thanks for being such a good sport. I had a feeling you were high quality."

To her dismay, Celia felt her stomach turn a small flip at his casually uttered words. "Really?" Despite her best intentions, a trace of mirth crept into her voice. "What was it, my sunny outlook? My incredible social grace?"

"I have no idea." Marcus sounded as if he, himself, were amazed. "But there's one thing I *do* know." He spoke with great conviction. "I get the feeling you're one woman I will never forget."

$\mathcal{S}ix$

"I have learned to look on nature, not as in the hour of
thoughtless youth; but hearing often times
The Still, sad music of humanity"
William Wordsworth

Ugh!" Celia struggled through the kitchen, her arms laden with the stack of crinkled magazines Marcus had dumped into the front seat of her white coupe.

Through the doorway to the sun-drenched living room, Hank watched, unperturbed, from his vantage point on a sagging sofa of wine-colored frisé.

Celia grunted. "Big help you are."

Obviously reveling in his indolence, the dog blinked, rolled onto his back, and drifted back to sleep.

Celia plopped the stack down on a turn-of-the-century cherry-wood bench and decided to make herself a cup of tea. As she poured tap water into an acid green-colored kettle, she reflected on Marcus's edict for the upcoming cover story: 'Top Five Inns of Sierra Nevada.'

"Great. I can't wait to see what other topics he's hit. Maybe 'New Summer Styles for Today's Fashionable Camper' or an article on dangerous cosmetic/enzyme combinations; 'Moisturizer,

Sunscreen, and You: Beware the Triple Threat,'" she grumbled. "Huhh. Better make this coffee. *Strong* coffee. It may be tough to stay awake."

Ten minutes later, Celia settled onto the sofa beside Hank, her feet tucked comfortably against the scratchy frisé, and drew a bright, sunflower-patterned quilt over her lap. She drank deeply from the rich black liquid in her mug and pulled a magazine from the top of the stack.

March 1985. The slick cover identified the issue's feature articles: 'Paradise Lost,' 'Marks of the Gold Rush,' an excerpt from John Muir's 'My First Summer in the Sierra.' Celia flipped through the pages, noting with surprise the top-quality photography and cutting-edge graphic design. One bold headline caught her attention, and she began to scan the text.

PARADISE LOST

In 1971, a brilliant, heart-wrenching story by the internationally-acclaimed Ted Geisel—better known as 'Dr. Seuss'—entered the literary marketplace, where it was received by rave reviews from children and ecologists alike. Boys and girls, scientists and environmentalists, were captivated by the haunting tale of the pitiful, all-too-familiar, greed-driven Once-ler and the valiant, stumpy defender of the defenseless: The Lorax.

Devoted to the preservation of "rippulous" ponds filled with Humming-Fish, singing Swomee-Swans, and of course, "…those trees! Those trees! Those Truffula Trees!" our sentimental hero set out to prevent their destruction by avaricious opportunists. In a realistic, yet amazingly nonchildlike story twist, The Lorax illustrated what far too many of us have

learned through painful experience—sadly, even the most elo-
quent words often fall on deaf ears.

Of course, The Lorax is set "Way back in the days when
the grass was still green and the pond was still wet and the
clouds were still clean...." Certainly, it is not a contemporary
tale; we are clearly dealing with a work of fiction. Yet in light
of our century's dark history, the struggle of the Lorax appears
to be not so extreme—not quite so unbelievable—after all.

Within the Sierra Nevada, several miles north of Yosemite's
Merced Canyon lies an adjacent river gorge, the Grand
Canyon of the Tuolumne, whose imposing fissure rivals that of
its mighty twin to the south. Resplendent with rushing water-
falls and lush, edible grasses, known to the Miwoks as
"Hatchatchie," the ravine once presented a picture-perfect
image of the idyllic mountain paradise.

Despite her earlier skepticism, Celia found herself captivated
by the story. As she read, she imagined she could hear Marcus's
voice reciting each line of copy with the same passion he had
expressed during his earlier description of the local landscape.

Camping parties first hiked in to the awe-inspiring
canyon in the 1890s. But friendly relations between man and
valley were woefully short-lived. The men and women who
actually witnessed firsthand the beauty of the Tuolumne
Canyon were pitifully few; in the early 1900s, the city of San
Francisco cast its eye upon the river as the long-term source of
the city's water supply. Hetch Hetchy Valley, within the
Tuolumne Canyon, was sentenced to internment as the site of
the controversial reservoir.

The article was illustrated by dramatic black-and-white photos of the first camping parties to Tuolumne, as well as contemporary shots of an impressive-looking dam.

Hetch Hetchy was not without her own Lorax. Rushing to her defense were naturalist John Muir and the politically active Sierra Club. When informed about the city's plans, an enraged Muir protested, "Dam Hetch Hetchy! As well dam for water tanks the people's cathedrals and churches, for no holier temple has ever been consecrated by the heart of man."

Supporters argued from every conceivable angle: There was no legal precedent supporting the Department of the Interior's decision to grant National Park property to a city for its own private use; a number of equally advantageous reservoir sites were available outside the boundaries of Yosemite; the beautiful meadow around Hetch Hetchy would ultimately better serve as a site for public recreation.

Yet despite such valiant efforts, all appeals were ignored, and in 1915, construction of the dam began.

As she examined the photos that chronicled the intrusion of man, Celia felt herself becoming increasingly indignant. She could imagine Marcus himself storming, unannounced, into city offices, begging...no, *demanding* that officials find an alternative course of action.

Amazingly, the invasion of Hetch Hetchy was merely the tip of the iceberg.

Over the mountains, on the eastern side of the Sierra, waged 'The Fight at the Water Hole,' what would one day be known as 'the rape of Owens Valley'; at its mildest, a battle more vitriolic than the worst skirmishes in the Hetch Hetchy dispute ever threatened to be.

Owens Valley had originally been settled by cattlemen in 1861. But it quickly became clear that the land was highly responsive to irrigation, and by the early 1900s, Inyo County was covered with bountiful orchards bearing apples, pears, peaches, and nuts. It was clearly a rousing success in the story of man's western advance.

In response to the valley's prosperity, the newly-established federal Reclamation Service deemed it wise to invest in an extensive irrigation system. Left in charge of the project was a man who had ties with the Los Angeles Department of Water and Power. Subsequent information leaks eventually led to the seizing of Inyo County water by Los Angeles.

City officials stubbornly insisted that their intent was simply to make use of excess water not needed by Owens Valley ranchers. Yet, at the time, the director of the Department of Water and Power was quoted as warning one land-speculator friend, "Do not go into Inyo County. We are going to turn that county dry."

And so, they did. Soon, residents of Owens Valley found themselves with no means of financial support, and with no choice but to leave their homes. Frustrated and angered, they demanded compensation from the city of Los Angeles.

Their pleas were ignored.

The next 20 years in Inyo County were marked by violence, suicides, vigilante attacks, and finally, seizure of the aqueduct's gates; in the end, residents accepted their defeat. Summing it up best were two headlines from a 1925 supplement to The Inyo Register and The Owens Valley Herald:

'GREED OF CITY RUINS THE OWENS VALLEY,' and 'LOSS OF BUSINESS AND PRESTIGE HAS COME TO CITY'S VERY DOORS.' The booming local economy inevitably collapsed, and today Owens Lake still stands dry.

Hetch Hetchy and Owens Valley are merely two in a long history of controversies detailing man's struggle to manage the environment. As we march toward a new century, we look back on the lessons of a previous generation and learn. But why bring up today the sins of an earlier generation? Because the story is far from over. The effects of such short-sighted action become increasingly apparent with each passing day.

In the Hetch Hetchy Valley, a net of penstocks, power lines, dams, powerhouses, and aqueducts mar the landscape, effectively illustrating for man the web in which we have entrapped ourselves.

In the saga of the Owens Valley water grab, the Los Angeles Department of Water and Power has for years diverted the streams that feed Mono Lake, threatening this unique salt lake and its entire ecosystem. At risk is not only this unusual high-desert inland sea, but also the Mono Lake Brine Shrimp and countless numbers of ducks, geese, swans, gulls, grebes— nearly 100 species of water birds—largely dependent on feeding at Mono Lake for their very survival.

Despite the still-present damage, in places like Mono Lake, one fact remains encouraging: Nearly 100 years after the conservation movement first began at Hetch Hetchy, concerned and aware citizens continue in their efforts to protect the interests of the wilderness in the tug-of-war between wise stewardship of resources and the gluttony of man.

In 1983, the California Supreme Court ruled that the "public trust" doctrine which first appeared in early Roman *law is applicable today to the issues at Mono Lake. This land-mark ruling determined that: "The state has an affirmative duty to take the public trust into account in the planning and allocation of water resources, and to protect public trust uses whenever feasible." This ruling superseded an earlier water code which ruled that "the use of water for domestic purposes is the highest use of water."*

Furthermore, in July 1984, after years of pleas by con-cerned citizens, the House of Representatives passed a bill that established the Mono Basin National Forest Scenic Area, which halted quartz mining in the area and authorized a study by the National Academy of Sciences on the effects of water diversions on the Mono Basin. What happens next? It is too early to know for sure. However, it is not inconceivable that the state could prevent further diversions from the Mono Basin. Only time will tell.

Such developments may be seen as a good sign; that an increasing number of citizens—regardless of political affilia-tion or philosophical background—are uniting in efforts to preserve our resources. Despite such efforts, it is doubtful that the havoc wreaked in our century will ever be completely reversed. Yet—amazingly—that may not be a bad thing across the board. For the signs that remain will always remind us of the Lorax's warning: "UNLESS someone like you cares a whole awful lot, nothing is going to get better. It's not."

When we see the results of man's destructive behavior, we are reminded that it is up to us to care 'a whole awful lot.' If we follow up such feelings with responsible actions, then there really is hope. Things can get better. And that would mean the world to men like John Muir, to the 'Lorax' in every man, woman and child who cares about the incredible world we were given.

Most of all, it will make a difference to the world itself, to future generations who will inhabit and enjoy it and, we can only hope, to the One who made it long ago...the Creator who brings life and beauty to all He touches.

Celia laid down the magazine and sat for a moment in silence. She shook her head in amazement. "Whew!" *This isn't a rag at all. It's actually pretty substantial.* She perused the stack of magazines beside her. Each headline seemed as issue-oriented as the one before: "Which Political Candidates Are Good Environmental Stewards?"; "'Drive-Through' Yosemite: Commercialization Hits America's National Parks."

As she scanned the articles, she became more and more impressed with her editor's obvious talent and intelligence. Despite her earlier frustration, she felt herself warming slightly to the man who had written with such passion. And she was embarrassed that she had allowed her feathers to be ruffled so easily.

She was halfway through December 1989 when she heard the jaunty beat of *shave-and-a-haircut, six bits* being pounded on her door. Celia smiled at the sound that, like "Chopsticks" plunked out on a piano, always made her feel—if only for a moment—like a carefree child once again. She crossed the room eagerly and opened the door.

Raising his eyes to her face, Marcus Stratton moved his lips, but no sound came forth. Looking startled, he remained in the doorway for several moments without speaking. His eyes focused on her tousled, dark hair, moved to her scruffy white T-shirt, then her battered navy sweat pants and thick wool socks.

51

Uncomfortable under his gaze, she moved back a step.

"Uh—," he stammered. "You shouldn't just open the door like that without finding out who it is."

Celia's eyes did not waver. "I knew it was you," she said simply.

"That's crazy. How could you know it was me?"

"I…just had a feeling. Besides, who else would know I was here? You're about the only person in Lundy who even knows I exist."

"Still. You should be more careful," he muttered. "May I come in?"

Celia motioned Marcus forward and led him toward the box-lined living room. "Please. Have a seat." She watched her guest closely, unsure of how to act. Although she was initially pleased to see him, she felt herself becoming increasingly nervous in the face of his awkward behavior. "Sorry about the mess. I haven't had a chance to unpack yet."

Marcus settled himself on an overstuffed chair and glanced around the room. "Is this all there is? You didn't bring much."

She shrugged. "I'm not staying long. The rest is in storage."

"Of course," Marcus mumbled absently. He reached across the coffee table and flipped through the pages of December 1989. "So…" Relieved, he seemed to grasp at a natural opportunity for conversation. "What do you think of *High Sierra* so far?"

"I think—," Celia settled herself beside Hank on the sofa. "I think what you've written is wonderful," she said with feeling. "You've got to be making a difference in the world with pieces like these. I just don't understand—," she faltered.

"What?" Marcus prodded. "Go ahead. I can take it."

"Well—I can't help but wonder, what's with the tourist bit? Top Five Inns? I don't get it. It's a shame to be so shallow in your anniversary issue." She glanced up at Marcus, who was staring at her. Celia pinched the bridge of her nose, as if fending off an oncoming headache. "Sorry. It's not my job to judge. I know you're paying me to shoot it, not to like it. And despite everything I said, I really do appreciate the work. I guess I just feel out of sorts today—"

"There's no need to apologize. A year ago I would have agreed with you." As Marcus spoke, he leaned forward and stared deeply into Celia's eyes. "About the article. But this isn't a year ago. Things are different now. I appreciate the advice, but I have to do what I have to do." The words were spoken gently, but his message was clear: End of discussion.

"Of course." Celia tore her eyes from his and stared down at her feet, feeling small and fragile, like a wounded bird.

Marcus rose from the chair and moved to the opposite end of the couch, closer to Celia, yet still an arm's length away. Hank shifted positions, grumbling briefly at the disturbance, then resumed his comfortable, sleepy wheeze.

"Look, I'm sorry," Marcus offered, absently stroking the animal's back. "I didn't come over here to shoot you down. There's a lot of wisdom in what you're saying. I'm just not in a position to do anything about it."

"Why *did* you come?"

The words were innocently spoken, but Marcus pulled back, as if under interrogation.

"Well…someone needs to make sure you're settling in all right, that you have everything you need," he said, his voice sounding a little loud. "We're responsible for bringing you here.

And, after our rough start, I thought it might be a good idea for that person to be me. I suppose I should have brought a fruit basket or something?" He glanced down helplessly at his rough, suntanned hands, empty except for a few strands of dog hair.

Celia laughed. "I'm not *sick,* for goodness sake! Anyway, it's the thought that counts...or something like that."

"In that case, I *thought* about stocking your entire pantry and cooking you the most incredible meal of your life." Marcus kept his face straight, but his eyes were laughing.

"What a guy." Celia raised her eyebrows in disbelief.

"You got that right."

"Watch it, bub," she warned. "I just might call your bluff."

"Oh, really?" The editor leaned forward and grinned. "Dinner? You and me?"

"Well, not tonight," Celia backpedaled. "I think Hank and I can fend for ourselves. But you really shouldn't make an offer like that unless you're prepared to follow through."

"Oh, I'm prepared," Marcus promised in a low voice. "Just try me."

Celia rose from the couch nervously. "Yes. Well...thanks for stopping by. But it's getting pretty late, and I want to get an early start in the morning."

"Very industrious of you. I'm sure your boss would be thrilled to hear it." Marcus seemed reluctant, but he followed her lead and stood.

"Yes, well, my *client* doesn't know what a good thing he's got." She laughed, laying one hand on Marcus's back and pushing him toward the door.

Marcus glanced back over his shoulder and smiled. "Good

night, Celia," he said, his voice soft and low.

"Good night, Marcus." Celia shut the door firmly behind him. Leaning her back against the solid wood frame, she listened as his footsteps trailed away down the driveway. Moments later, an engine roared to life and Marcus sped off into the night.

"Now, *that* was a strange visit." She relived the unexplainable rush of pleasure she had felt at finding Marcus standing on her front porch. "The question is—," Celia addressed the brown and white body lying motionless on the sofa, "do we like him or not?" She plopped down beside the animal and eyed him critically. "Look at you. You're not even listening. You've got me talking to *myself* now. Thanks a lot." Her tone softened as Hank rolled over and whined softly. "That's okay. You've got a lot of other redeeming qualities. You haven't a shallow, disloyal bone in your whole pudgy little body." Celia prodded a layer of dog fat with her index finger, then buried her face in the rough fur on Hank's back. "And you love your mom more than anything in the world. Isn't that so?"

Hank raised his head and happily nudged Celia's face with his runny, black muzzle. She drew the animal close against her chest, ignoring the offensive smell of his breath. "All right, all right, you adorable mutt. That's it. I don't care *what* Valerie says. Tonight you're getting pizza."

Seven

❧

*"...love must have some future, and
for us there were only moments."*
Albert Camus, *La Peste*

For her first day of work, Celia decided to head south to the Silver Lake Honeymoon Lodge. The outside shots alone held great promise. Located a few miles off I-395, the knotty-pine cabin stood only one hundred feet from the most spectacular body of water on the June Lake Loop. At an elevation of over seven thousand feet, the glacial waters had been a successful trout fishing spot for decades. More recently, awestricken couples from bordering western states had spread the word about the lake's serenity and natural beauty, and the site's popularity as a honeymoon retreat had grown dramatically.

Expensive vacation homes dotted the hillside. Within minutes of turning off the highway, Celia found herself motoring along the lake's northwest shore, snatching quick glimpses of sunlight skipping across a surface like sapphire-colored glass. Soon she passed a small cluster of charming, rustic cabins. Reflecting upon Marcus's directions, Celia estimated that she had only another two miles to travel before coming upon the lodge.

She glanced unhappily at the empty bucket seat beside her.

Normally, Hank traveled with her on the job, but then, most shoots took place outdoors where he could do little harm. Although she hated to leave him home, alone and bored, she'd chosen to do so for this assignment. It seemed logical that most proprietors would prefer not to have her furry companion traipsing about their inns, leaving trails of short tan and white hairs as evidence of his presence. Earlier, at the office, Celia had laughed when Eva referred to Hank as a "latchkey dog." Now, as she thought of him back at the house, she felt guilty and out of sorts.

Following her notes, Celia made the designated turnoff, crept down a narrow gravel driveway, and parked in front of a two-story log dwelling nestled close to the rocky shore.

"All right…let's get this over with." She grabbed her light meter and trudged toward the tiny lodge. Beneath her feet, a white stone path led through a sea of wood chips to a gabled, river-rock entrance. From window boxes at either side of the door, crimson wildflowers nodded in greeting with each breath of wind.

Celia pulled out the key Eva had given her, unlocked the front door, and pushed it open.

"Hello?" Silence echoed back from the heavy pine-log walls. As she had anticipated, the house was empty. With no one on-site to cook, the small cabin was not a true "bed and breakfast," as were the other featured inns. Yet, for a bride and groom seeking solitude and privacy, the circumstances could not be any more ideal.

Celia had expected to find herself standing in a dark, "cozy" living area; she discovered instead a sunny, spacious sitting room with walls of hand-hewn pine. The room extended nearly forty feet across, and fourteen-foot-high beams arched across the ceiling. On the large stone hearth lay a pile of freshly cut wood, ready to be kindled into welcoming flames.

Two antique bookcases stood along the outside walls, over-flowing with volumes of classic poetry and literature. Celia stepped close to one of the shelves and turned a worn cover, fingering the fragile, onion paper of Rossetti's *House of Life*. Beneath her feet, a hunter-green rug lay over polished hardwood floors, complementing the room's plaid roll-armed sofa and navy gingham chairs. Along the walls hung a collection of gilt-framed botanicals: jacinth, cinnamon rose, tawny narcissus. The cornucopia of colors came full circle with drapes of scarlet tapestry.

Feeling her heavy mood begin to lighten within the room's friendly atmosphere, Celia pulled a list from her pocket. "Okay, let's see...boss man wants shots of the lake at sunset, the high-beamed sitting room, and the honeymoon suite. Piece of cake." She moved toward the heavy timber stairs to explore the loft.

At the top of the steps, Celia paused to survey the romantic bridal suite before her. Directly across from the stairwell stood the room's centerpiece—a great, intricately-carved, maple sleigh bed, adorned by a cream-colored chenille comforter and colorful embroidered pillows. Beneath the bed lay a beige Chinese petit point rug, and white eyelet curtains swept the window panes, positioned perfectly to protect guests from the glare of the early morning sun.

What do young couples think when they stand in this spot? Celia wondered. *Are they frightened by the commitment they've just made? Are they worried about the future? Or are all other thoughts pushed aside by the joy of being held within their lover's arms?*

Trying to escape further sentimental feelings, Celia peeked through a doorway at her left, which opened into the master bath—white porcelain basin, drawstring toilet, claw-foot tub, sandstone tiles. Behind the door hung two thick terry cloth robes; His and Hers. Celia wistfully fingered the soft white cloth.

Paul and I never got to come to a place like this. Now we never will.

In the two years that handsome, spirited financier Paul Kellum was a part of Celia's life, they had never gone away on a romantic weekend together. Although Celia had loved Paul with all of her being, she'd known better than to suggest such a get-away. To have done so would have signaled more than she was willing to give. And unwilling to risk a course of action that could ultimately lead to uncomfortable entanglements, Paul himself had never brought up the subject.

Steering clear of Paul's bed had not been a conscious decision of morality for Celia; she had ceased in her efforts to please others by "being good" shortly after her parents died. Yet somehow, the idea of spending the night with Paul had seemed like a step out of sequence.

I haven't stopped believing in fairy tales, she'd rationalized. *And I'm not ready to give up my dream yet. The first time I wake up in his arms, I want it to be as his wife...not as a woman he could live without.*

Celia stepped back through the doorway and crossed to the bedroom window where she gazed out at the white-capped peaks. It was nearly two years ago now, upon a mountain much like the Sierra, that Paul and several friends had tried to teach her how to ski. After two hours on the "bunny" slopes and four aborted attempts to board the ski lift, Celia had finally managed to make it to the top of the mountain. However, the snow was icy, her snowplowing skills weak, and within less than a minute she had landed face-down at the top of the trail, her legs pointed awkwardly in opposite directions. Despite the agonizing pressure on her knees, she had laughed hysterically at the sight of Paul staring openmouthed at her prone figure.

"Help!" she giggled through the pain. "I've fallen and I can't get up!"

Paul rolled his eyes in feigned disgust. "You're pathetic. Really pitiful." Yet heedless of the disruption of his own vacation, he had pulled her from the snow, obtained first aid for her torn ligaments, and nursed her with hot cocoa and Scrabble for the remainder of the weekend while their companions explored the alpine trails.

If that's not love, I don't know what is. During their first year together, Celia had seen signs of love in every interaction. Yet even as their friendship and passion grew, for every two steps of progress made in their relationship, Paul took at least one step back.

"Sweetheart, I love you. Honestly, I do. But marriage?" So clearly was the sound of Paul's voice imprinted in her mind, Celia could almost imagine that he stood beside her once more. "I'm just not sure. You wouldn't want me to make a decision like that without being sure?"

"Paul, we've been dating seriously for two years. If you're not sure by now, when are you ever going to be sure?"

His silence was his answer.

Celia had fought to maintain composure but was unable to keep the tears from her eyes. "Paul, I can't go on like this forever. Something's got to give. Either you love me, or you don't. If you love me, then *love* me! And if you don't, just say so, and I'll go. If you don't want to be with me, then I need to get on with my life."

Paul shook his head angrily. "I don't like ultimatums. If you want to go, then go. Nobody's stopping you."

"I guess that's true." As he turned away, Celia closed her eyes in anguish. *If he loves me, he'll come back. He'll fight for me. He won't let me go.* Paul had stormed out of the room in frustration then, without bidding her good-bye. It wasn't the first time they'd had that conversation, but it was the last.

Standing alone in the honeymoon suite, Celia lifted a long-stemmed daisy from a crystal vase on the bureau, and with one long, slow motion, drew the petals along her cheek. There were daisies at the funeral. It was one of the moments she remembered best—sitting in the front pew of the church, numbering their bright, sunny faces. *One, two, three....* Celia was aware that a preacher was speaking but was unable to hear his voice over the noise in her head. *Thirty-seven, thirty-eight, thirty-nine....* Was somebody singing? *Fifty-four, fifty-five, fifty-six....* Seventy-four daisies had given their lives in memorial of a man who had never understood the importance of sending flowers.

"Enough!" Celia's voice sounded shaky, and much too loud, in the stillness of the house. Passing a cotton sleeve across the dampness in her eyes, she pushed all thoughts of Paul from her mind. As she fled the room and the memories it had triggered, a single white blossom lay where it had been dropped at the baseboard, left to wither and fade, abandoned and alone.

Eight

❧

"'Would you tell me please, which way I ought to go from here?'
'That depends a good deal on where you want
to get to,' said the Cat.'"
Lewis Carroll, *Alice in Wonderland*

Celia strolled along Sonora Avenue, breathing in the sweet scent of roadside juniper. Her eyes flickered first to the animal trotting ahead, then to the lopsided buildings along her path. With a population of less than one thousand, Lundy seemed like a child whose growth was stunted. Basic services were available: doctor and dentist, beauty salon, gas station, drugstore and grocery. But though the small town may once have been poised to join the sorority of booming California cities, this former debutante now seemed tired and worn.

Several buildings had been renovated and lovingly refurbished, with fresh wood and paint covering a variety of wounds. But attempts at a facelift appeared to have been, for the most part, halfhearted. Still, Lundy faced the world bravely, with a singular style Celia thought of as 'Historical Tacky.' Despite the lack of traditional beauty, Celia felt drawn to the dusty streets, so unlike the fast-food strips of Anytown, U.S.A. So far from home.

"Hey, stranger! Wait up!"

Celia looked up in surprise as a graceful, athletic-looking woman bounced across the street.

"Hey, yourself! What are you doing here?" Even as the words came out of Celia's mouth, the answer became obvious as Valerie jogged over to her.

"I'm out for my morning run."

"Ugh!" Celia wrinkled her nose in disgust and continued walking. "An early riser! How do you do it?"

"What do you mean? You're up." Valerie slowed her pace to match Celia's.

"Yes. But not by *choice*." Celia indicated the moving brown and white lump ahead. "I have to do something with Mr. Excess Energy. Hank can't go with me on my photo shoots, so I'm trying to get him some exercise and relieve my guilt—"

"Why can't he go with you on the trail?"

Celia rolled her eyes and brought her friend up to date as they walked. "So it looks like I'll be shooting muffins and eggs, not mountaintops and eagles," she finished.

"I'm sorry. You must be terribly disappointed."

"Oh, I was. But I'm getting used to the idea." Celia shrugged. "It's work. And…it got me out of Atlanta," she said absently, her eyes on the hills.

Valerie continued along in silence. After a moment she remarked casually, "That's not the first time you've mentioned getting a fresh start. It sounds like you really wanted to get out of there."

Celia broke out of her reverie to tune in on the conversation. "Well, you know how it is. A place gets old after awhile—"

Valerie shook her head. "I don't think that's it. You're running from something, aren't you? Celia, are you in trouble?"

"No." Celia turned away uncomfortably. "It's nothing like that."

Valerie grasped at her sleeve and pulled her to a halt. "All right, then." Her voice was soft. "What *is* it like?"

"What difference does it make?" Celia stared stubbornly at her shoes.

"It obviously makes a difference to you."

"Why do you care?" Celia's voice held an ill-concealed trace of bitterness.

"Because I like you." Valerie squeezed her arm gently.

"You hardly know me."

"True," Valerie allowed. "But I like what I see. I think you remind me of myself, a little."

Celia looked up, surprised. "You poor thing."

Val laughed. "I could say the same thing!"

The two began to walk again, and Valerie kindly stopped probing for the moment.

"You know, it's funny," Celia ventured finally. "When I first started doing freelance work, it seemed like a hassle to be living in Atlanta. I couldn't have been based much further from the heart of things. But I couldn't imagine living anywhere else." She felt the pain even as she talked. "Then things changed in my life, and I couldn't imagine staying. All I knew was that I wanted to get away. And now, here I am. I'm in a new place, with new faces…and I don't know what to do with myself! I don't feel comfortable with people anymore…I don't know how to act or where to go from here."

"The world's a big place," Valerie commented. "And it

sounds like you have no ties. My guess is, a footloose single woman like yourself could probably go any place, do anything. It just depends on what you want."

"I think I just want…to be safe." The words were quietly spoken.

Hazel eyes peered at her intently. "That's a valid thing to want. Do you feel safe here?"

"I…think so. For now. It's why I came," Celia said simply.

Valerie looked concerned. "Are you sure no one's after you?"

"Oh, no. I'm not in any physical danger, or anything like that… ."

"Then what?"

Celia sighed. "Let's just say it's been a rough couple of years." Her voice held a hint of warning.

"I see." She paused, then seemed to search for something to say. "It sure would be nice if we could just hop in the car and drive to someplace where we would never get hurt."

"You can say *that* again," Celia agreed emphatically.

"I think that's why I'm not afraid of dying."

"What?" Celia turned to stare at her.

Valerie shrugged. "I think heaven must be a place where we are all…well, like you said. Safe."

Celia looked unconvinced. "That's a nice thought. Too bad it isn't a lot of help here and now."

"Well, I guess that depends on where you're standing. Heaven doesn't feel so far away to me."

"It sounds like you're a pretty spiritual person."

"We're all spiritual people," Valerie said cryptically.

"Not me." Celia came to a stop and set her heels.

Valerie paused beside her, and stared intently into Celia's eyes. "*You*, Celia Randall, are a *very* spiritual woman. Isn't that what we've been talking about all this time? Questions of the spirit and the heart?" She raised a hand to her brow, shielding her eyes from the sun's glare, and pointed down the street toward her office. "I'm afraid I've got to go. I've got an 8:00 A.M. appointment. Maybe I'll see you later?"

Celia nodded uncertainly.

"All right. Well, good luck on your shoot. And, Celia—" Valerie gave her sleeve a sisterly tug. "If you need someone to talk to, or just to hang out with, give me a call, okay? We all need friends—if we're going to feel safe."

Valerie picked up her pace, and as Celia watched, the other woman turned and ran off down the street, soon becoming nothing more than a bobbing speck in the distance.

Nine

❧

"Making peace is harder than making war."
Adlai Stevenson, Speech, 1951

Tires crunched against gravel as the Mustang crossed honey-colored fields, once the feeding ground for local herds. Celia peered through her bug-spattered windshield and regarded the peculiar dwelling directly ahead.

There was no mistaking its origin; with its vaulted roof, painted red board-and-bat walls, and white trim, the structure could not have met more perfectly the specifications of a traditional country barn. Marcus's notes indicated that it was built early in the century by a wealthy rancher. Sierra land had never enjoyed great farming success; at best, it provided summer ranges for cattle and sheep. But one stubborn Texas cowhand had fought to maintain his homestead until the early forties. After the main house burned down, the land remained abandoned for nearly thirty years before the current owners obtained the deed and immersed themselves in their vast remodeling project. The result was one of the most unusual bed and breakfasts in the Sierra.

Celia parked her car near the main entrance, cut the engine, and stared at the building before her. Against the background of low-lying hills thick with conifer forests, the barn stood out, bright and cheerful, an element of contrast like a brightly painted buoy bobbing in waters of deep green.

As she walked toward the building, Celia noticed that skylights had been installed in the lower sections of the shingled roof, letting in an optimum measure of sun. At the very top, a tiny, graceful cupola supported the structure's heavy iron weather vane. Oversized barn doors functioned as the main entry; above them, the original hayloft stood open, wide and welcoming.

Celia tapped timidly on the front door. When she received no immediate response, she turned the dew-covered knob beneath her fingers and gave a small push. The heavy door swung easily on its hinges, allowing her access into a small waiting area obviously designed for guest registration. A tall oak desk stood unattended, and the reservation book lay open.

Beyond the small sitting room, Celia spied one of the most enormous living areas she had ever seen. Along the right wall was a great forge built of wrought iron and river rocks, now converted into a fireplace that was the inn's main heat source. The blue-and-white ticking couch was flanked by two colorful floral-print chairs. Celia breathed in deeply as the smell of grilled cinnamon bread wafted from a doorway at the back of the room.

"Hello?" she called.

An older woman, tall and graceful, with small, pointed features appeared in the doorway. Her ash-blonde hair was pulled back into a loose French braid, and a crimson, gauzelike skirt flowed from beneath a starched white apron. Suede earth shoes covered wool-stockinged feet.

"Hullo!" Her eyes were wide and bright. "Sorry, have you been here long? I didn't hear you. We're in a bit of a tizzy over breakfast and not used to getting folks in this early. You must be the photographer Marcus sent?" She wiped her hands on her apron and moved to welcome her visitor.

"Celia Randall. Please, don't let me interrupt you...Mrs. Knapp?" Hazel eyes met her own green ones, and the two women shook hands warmly.

"Felicia."

Celia smiled. "Felicia. Eva said that you and your husband have graciously agreed to make two breakfasts today: one for your guests, and one for our shoot. That's very kind of you."

"Whatever it takes! It's just good business, exposure like this. Besides, we'd do anything for Marcus. Isn't that right, Charlie? Charlie?" She leaned back into the kitchen and sniffed. "Charlie! The potatoes!" A look of panic swept over her face.

Celia stepped back and waved her arms in dismissal. "Felicia, please don't worry about me! I'd prefer to take my outside shots first, anyway, while the lighting's better. There's no rush on brunch. Really."

With a look that communicated eternal gratitude, the proprietress slipped back through the doorway and was out of sight before her guest had even finished speaking.

Celia yawned and glanced at her watch: 6:45. Perfect. She should have at least three hours of good lighting—plenty of time to finish up what she needed before moving indoors.

Outside she began to explore the rambling, sunny rock garden, abundant with wildflowers: showy columbine, rosy paintbrush, and fiery shooting stars. As Celia walked, she stopped every few steps to measure light samples or assess the composition possibilities of an individual bud, blade, or stem. Taking in deep breaths of the fresh mountain air, her body began to relax, and she found herself in her element for the first time since arriving in Lundy.

After nearly an hour of analysis, Celia began to shoot. Working deliberately but quickly, she managed to finish off four rolls of film before the sun rose high overhead and removed the shadows necessary to give her photos depth. She glanced at her wrist watch. Half past ten.

"Whew!" Celia always lost herself in her art. Normally, she spent her midmorning break entertaining Hank; instinctively, she moved to scan the surrounding landscape for his form. But even as she turned, she remembered he was at home, moping. So she was surprised to discover someone waiting for her after all. A figure stood about two hundred feet away, quietly observing.

"Stratton? Is that you?"

The figure began to amble forward.

Celia took a deep breath and wiped her sweaty palms against her faded Levi's. Despite the warmth of the morning sun, she felt suddenly chilled in her sleeveless, blue poplin work shirt and rubbed her arms briskly.

"What are you doing here?" she asked testily as he drew near.

"Fine. Thanks for asking," Marcus bantered. "It's good to see you again, too." Standing before her in his green jersey polo, cotton shorts, and scruffy moccasins, he looked almost boyish, yet at the same time, even more bronzed and masculine than she had remembered.

"Sorry." Celia forced herself to sound apologetic. "I'm afraid I'm not very social when I'm working. Was there something you needed?"

"Actually, no. I was just coming to see if there was anything *you* needed. I'm heading down to Mammoth Lakes this afternoon. They've got the best photography facilities in the area. I thought I could maybe pick up some supplies for you and drop off whatever film you have ready for developing."

"Oh." Celia's embarrassment was genuine. "That was...thoughtful of you. Just give me a minute to unload." As she rewound her film, she mentally kicked herself. *Open mouth...insert foot. You're a real charmer, C. Excellent networking skills. Maybe now would be a good time to ask the man for a reference?*

"How are things going so far?"

"Why?" Celia's voice was suspicious.

"Oh, c'mon!" Marcus shook his head and ran his fingers through his hair, his frustration clearly showing. "What's with you anyway? It doesn't matter what I say, you're always ready for battle. Maybe I want to help you with your job. Maybe I'm just interested in you. Is that so bad?"

Celia stared, not knowing what to say.

Marcus sighed. "For the last time, I'm *sorry* about the dog, and I'm *sorry* I pulled that joke on you. But obviously, you've made up your mind to hate me. I might as well just leave you alone. Give the film to Eva when you're ready, and I'll take it in later this week." He turned away and started back toward the house.

"Wait!" The sound of her voice surprised even Celia. He stopped in his tracks and rotated to face her. "Mammoth Lakes, huh? Uh...how long will you be gone?"

"Wha—?" Marcus looked confused. "Most of the afternoon. Why?"

"Well," Celia swallowed nervously. "I was just sort of thinking...I need a new filter, and I'm not sure what they've got.

Maybe I could come along and look for myself?"

"Sure, but—" Marcus's eyes held the question, *A minute ago, you were at my throat. Now you want to go for a ride? What happened between then and now?*

"Please," Celia offered no explanation. "I'm…sorry I've been difficult. Just don't be mad. I hate it when people leave mad." For a moment she felt strangely afraid of something.

"It's all right. No harm done."

"Good." Celia was relieved, and now that everything was okay again, she felt her guard go up.

"How much time do you need here?"

"Well, I need to find out how breakfast is coming. After I shoot that, I'm done for the day. I'll get some more inside shots when I come back tomorrow to photograph the duck pond. I was planning to finish this afternoon, but the clouds are rolling in." Celia shielded her eyes and peered up at the puffs above. "It will be too dark this afternoon to give me the color I need."

Marcus followed her gaze. "That's too bad," he acknowledged. "But I guess the ducks' loss is my gain! Now I've got company for my trip." He grinned cheerfully.

"Yeees," Celia agreed, already halfway regretting her decision. "Let's see how things are going inside."

A bouquet of tantalizing smells teased their noses as they walked through the door. Celia moved toward the Elizabethan sideboard in the dining area, her eyes widening in wonder at the abundant spread: amber hazelnut waffles with thick Marionberry syrup, Black Forest ham, steaming apple-walnut sausage, cornmeal cakes with fresh blueberry compote, golden fried potatoes, cinnamon-crusted coffee cake, cappuccino, and a pitcher of pulpy, fresh-squeezed orange juice.

Marcus looked delighted. "If she shoots it fast, can we eat it, Fee?"

Celia watched her employer plant a kiss on the cheek of their hostess.

"Don't worry, Marcus. I kept plenty warm for you once I got your call. Oh, yes—," she responded to Celia's raised eyebrow. "He phoned a little while ago asking if you were still here."

Marcus's face grew pink. "Well, sure," he explained. "I wanted to make sure I'd be able to pick up the film if I came all the way out here."

"Of course." Felicia looked skeptical. "Film. Well, like you asked, there's breakfast *for two* in the oven." She turned to Celia. "If there's anything else you need, please…just holler." With that, she disappeared into the kitchen.

Marcus looked at Celia sheepishly.

" 'Breakfast for two'! She's such a kidder. No, really…I just thought you might be hungry after working all morning. Don't worry. I didn't mean anything by it. Not a thing."

Curiously, Celia found herself feeling both relieved and faintly disappointed.

"Of course." Her voice was brisk. "Don't be silly. I never thought you did. I'm sure I'll be much too busy here to eat with you anyway." Celia clenched her abdominal muscles, hoping to silence the rumblings in her stomach.

"Oh. Right. Sure. That makes sense. I, uh…guess I'll just go grab a bite and say 'hi' to Charlie. If you're really nice to me, I may even save you a piece of sausage."

Celia rolled her eyes. "Oh, stop. You're spoiling me." She was rewarded by the appearance of Marcus's now-familiar grin.

"All right. Look, I don't want to interrupt you again. I'll slip out the back when I'm done and just meet you at the office at around…what? One-thirty?"

"Fine." Celia's stomach turned at the thought of the event now before her. *What have I done?*

"See you then."

"Yeah. See ya."

Celia turned back to the pile of food and concentrated on planning shots that would complete her task as quickly as possible. Something told her she'd need time to collect her thoughts and gather her strength before spending the entire afternoon with this ebullient, irritating man who, she was discovering, had such an overwhelming effect on her.

CHAPTER

Ten

❧

"Tell me not (Sweet) I am unkind."
Richard Lovelace, 'To Lucasta, Going to the Wars'

Celia fidgeted uncomfortably in the passenger seat. "What time do you think we'll get there?"

"You're kidding! Why didn't you go before we left?"

"Ha, ha. Oh, my aching sides," Celia deadpanned. "I'm serious. How long is the drive?"

"Hmm," Marcus considered. "I'd say about forty minutes. Why? Having second thoughts already? We can still turn back."

"Nooo." Celia would have liked nothing better, but she would never give Marcus the satisfaction of admitting that he unnerved her. "Just a lousy backseat driver, I guess."

"Huh," Marcus grunted.

They drove on in uncomfortable silence for several long minutes.

"So." Celia jumped at the sound of his voice. "How are you enjoying your work so far? Not too painful, I hope?"

"No," she admitted. "It's not that bad. Of course, it's not exactly what I had in mind—"

"Of course."

"—but it really hasn't been the letdown I thought it might be. The B & B's I've seen so far are really spectacular, and the Knapps are wonderful."

Marcus nodded. "Charlie worked with my grandfather at the Forest Service for over twenty years. Our families go way back. It's nice to be in a position to do something to help out him and Fee."

"Is that why you're doing it?" Celia questioned.

" 'Doing it'?"

"You know, the piece about the inns. It obviously doesn't fit your magazine." When Marcus did not immediately respond, she added lamely, "In the last ten years, you've covered everything from political candidates to acid rain. You can't tell me you actually care about a bunch of crummy inns."

"Crummy? You know, you've got a lot of nerve coming along and passing judgment on good people making an honest living." Celia could sense Marcus pulling back. And recently, that kind of response was one of *her* favorite tactics; it unnerved her to be on the receiving end.

"I didn't mean that *they* were crummy," she protested. "And I don't even think their inns are crummy, actually, when you get right down to it." She looked nervously at Marcus's angry profile. "It's just that the *topic* is so crummy, compared to what you normally do."

Marcus drove on in stormy silence.

"Oh, come on! Don't be like that. It's sort of a twisted compliment, when you think about it. I guess I just expected a lot. Isn't that a good thing?" When he failed to respond, she muttered quietly, "Well, *I* thought it was a good thing. Go ahead. Make it a rotten magazine. See if I care."

They continued on without speaking for several miles; to Celia, it seemed an eternity. She stared out the window, pouting. *What's his problem, anyway? All I did was ask a simple question. Sheesh. Mr. Touchy. You'd think he might care about what he's doing. He's the editor, after all. It's his job to care, not mine.* Despite all her best efforts to convince herself otherwise, Celia continued to feel that she could not let the subject go.

"Okay. Fine. I admit it. I *do* care," she finally broke into the quiet of the cab. Marcus tore his gaze from the road and glanced at her in surprise. "It's just that—why would you want to mess up a good thing? You've got a decent magazine going here," she appealed. "That's pretty rare."

"It's not as easy as it seems." Marcus struggled to find the right words.

"What? I didn't take you to be the sort of man who's put off by hard work."

"That's not what I meant by 'easy.' The publishing business is complicated...."

"*Obviously.*" Celia took a deep breath and made an effort to sweeten her acerbic tone. "Okay, what do you mean by 'complicated'?"

"I mean that what is *good* is not necessarily the same thing as *popular.*"

"Meaning?"

"Meaning, the market is only so big...there's only so much room on the racks for magazines like *High Sierra.*"

"And...?"

"And...there's a new kid in town. A big, rich kid. And his daddy owns the newsstand."

"Oooh." Celia let out her breath slowly.

"That's right. *Oh.* For years, this company has hung on by a thread. And now that it's finally starting to look like a viable business, some yahoo with a chip on his shoulder and money in his pockets is moving in on our territory. I wouldn't mind so much if the competition was someone decent." Marcus became agitated, his voice louder in tone. "But it's this guy Powell. All money, no depth. But he's going to make it. He's got the breaks. *We're* the ones who can't compete."

"What do you mean?" Celia argued. "From everything I've seen and heard, you've done a great job with the magazine."

"Thanks," Marcus responded wryly. "But a company needs more than a soapbox and some pretty pictures if it's going to make it in this business. *High Sierra* just doesn't have the same kind of resources—corporate financial support, high-level advertisers, access to big-business mailing lists. For years I've fought outside pressure to give the magazine a more 'popular' twist. Now, I've run out of options. If 'trendy' is what sells, then 'trendy' it'll have to be."

Celia sat quietly, deep in concentration. After several minutes, she spoke again. "Can I ask another question without getting my head bitten off?"

Marcus shrugged. "You can try."

"Whatever made you decide to start a magazine like this?"

"That's easy. I made a promise."

"What kind of promise?"

"To my grandfather. When I was a kid, my mother used to bring me out to Pops's cabin for spring and summer vacations. That man knew every square foot of these mountains! He took me everywhere—Mono Craters, Devil's Postpile, Half Dome,

Tuolumne Falls. He taught me to see the beauty in every growing, living thing—black oak, incense cedar, manzanita blossoms, flowering dogwood, azalea bushes.... He's the one who helped me understand nature's worth. Pops was very literate. He used to read to me from the works of John Muir—*'Nevermore, however weary, should one faint by the way who gains the blessings of one mountain day; whatever his fate, long life, short life, stormy or calm, he is rich forever.'"*

Celia nodded appreciatively. "That's exactly the way I feel when I'm out alone on a shoot—*rich*, as if I'm the only one who has access to that particular treasure. No matter how wonderful and majestic I imagine the world to be, it always turns out to be even more incredible than I had dreamed."

"'Wherever we go in the mountains, or indeed in any of God's wild fields, we find more than we seek.'"

"Let me guess. Muir?"

"Muir," Marcus assented.

"Hmm." Celia gave him a thoughtful sideways glance. "It's just that being out there, taking my photos, helps put everything back into perspective for me. No matter how bad things get, I can't help but feel like there's reason for hope when I see the new life that sprouts up in nature. At times, it makes me feel...happy to be alive."

"'Precious night, precious day to abide in me forever. Thanks be to God for this immortal gift.'"

Uncomfortable with this serious turn of conversation, Celia turned a mischievous eye on her chauffeur. "Stop quoting!" she demanded.

"Ah... *'The little Douglas is fiery, peppery, full of brag and fight and show....'"*

"I'll 'fight and show' you.…"

"Truce! Truce!" Marcus laughed and leaned away from her tiny raised fists. "I'm the driver, remember?"

"What was that crack about the *'little Douglas'*? Are you calling me a tree?"

"Muir again. He was talking about squirrels." Marcus adopted a pompous tone. "I think he would have likened me to *'the large California gray…shy…wishing only to be let alone apparently, and manifesting no desire to be seen or admired or feared.'*"

"Give me a break."

"That's not all. In fact, *'the California gray is one of the most beautiful…of our hairy neighbors.'*"

"I think I'm going to be carsick."

"Now, *you,* on the other hand, are more like *'the Douglas…the brightest of all the squirrels I have ever seen—'*"

"The brightest, huh? I'll buy that."

"*'—a hot spark of life, making every tree tingle with his prickly toes—'*"

"Watch it.…"

"*'—How he scolds, and what faces he makes.…If not so comically small, he would indeed be a dreadful fellow.…'*"

"Hey! You really *are* an ogre, aren't you?"

Marcus smirked contentedly. "If the hairy knuckles fit.…"

"All right, all right. So what about the promise?"

"Ah, yes…the promise. Well, one day, when I was still just a pup, Pops took me out on a nature walk at the end of a terrible storm. All morning I had listened to thunder reporting strike after strike of lightning. That afternoon we wandered through the forest, and I could see the marks of destruction—broken limbs, eroded topsoil, soggy piles of stripped pine needles. I knew that if we had been outside only an hour earlier, we would have been merely two more victims. As we walked, Pops talked to me about the two kinds of damage that can be done to the earth—that wrought by nature, which the world can survive, and that caused by man, which it often cannot."

A look of peace crept over Marcus's face as he expertly maneuvered the Land Cruiser through a series of difficult curves.

"I remember holding tightly to his rough, age-spotted hand, listening to the deep rumbling of his voice, and breathing in the sweet smell that comes only after a big rain. Suddenly we came to a small clearing, and as we stood surrounded by trees, three bright rays of sun shone through the clouds and into our meadow, followed by the appearance of a rainbow. That's the first time anyone explained to me the story of the rainbow and of God's promise. It was the greatest moment. Even as a kid, I knew it. I wanted to remember it always. So I asked, 'Make me a promise, Pops!' 'You first,' he said. And so I promised that when I grew up, I'd keep people from ruining the forest. I knew that would please him. 'That's a big promise' he warned me. 'That's okay,' I told him. 'I'm a big boy.'"

"How'd that go, again? *Manifesting no desire to be admired...?*"

"Well, I was just a rug-rat at the time. But point well taken."

"What did he promise you?"

"He said, 'Tell you what, son. I'll make you a bargain. You just be yourself. Try to do the best you can in life. And I promise I'll always love you, no matter what. Even after you think I'm gone.' The man always kept his word. That was how the dream got started for me. When Pops died ten years ago, he willed me his cabin. I'd been out of college for two years working at the city news desk in Sacramento. I took the little bit of money he left me, plus several thousand I begged off my parents, and started the magazine. It's been an uphill battle, but I feel like I've kept my promise."

"*Woodman, spare that tree! Touch not a single bough! In youth it sheltered me, And I'll protect it now.*'"

"Very good. George Pope Morris?"

Celia nodded. "*Are* you protecting it now?"

A look of irritation flickered in Marcus's eyes. "Now? Now, I'm in survival mode. I can't help anybody if I'm bankrupt."

"What would Pops say?"

"Pops isn't here, now is he?"

"But what about, 'Even after you think I'm gone…'?"

"I don't just *think* he's gone, Celia. I *know* he's gone. There's nothing he—or you—can do to help. So please, I'd appreciate it if you just kept any misguided attempts at reviving my conscience to yourself."

"Fine. There's no reason to get nasty."

Marcus let out a long breath. "Sorry. You're right. I have no right to take my problems out on you. Listen to me!" He sounded bewildered. "Never before have I had to apologize so many times in just a few days. Something about you must bring out the fighter in me."

"It's because I'm a prickly, peppery squirrel. Remember?"

"Maybe." Marcus seemed to give her explanation serious consideration. "Or maybe it's that I'm a selfish boor."

"Yeah, that's it," Celia agreed.

The two smiled timidly at one another.

"Truce?"

"Truce."

"Look. Up ahead." The appearance of several buildings along the horizon signified that it was time to end the battle.

"Well, Douglas, thanks for your company. Our conversation has been every bit as scintillating as I had anticipated."

"Really, Gray? You turned out to be quite a surprise. I imagined you'd be a real bore."

Marcus raised his eyebrows. "Well, of course. That's to be expected when you are as shy and retiring as I—"

"All right, all right," Celia cut him off as he slowed the vehicle and pulled onto a side street. "Let's park this heap and get this show on the road. You don't want to be late and worry the other trolls."

As they rolled to a stop, Marcus pulled on the emergency brake and turned to face her. To Celia, he seemed uncomfortably close as he gazed into her wide eyes.

"Look, Celia." A strange feeling came over her as, for the first time, he used her given name. "All kidding aside. I think you're an *incredible* woman." He said the word with feeling. "And I'd hate for you to believe that I really am an ogre. Please tell me that I'm off the hook here."

"Weeell. All right. You're forgiven." Celia tried to keep the mood light as Marcus took her small fingers in his and squeezed them warmly. "But don't get too cocky, now. I know where you work, and I'm not one to be trifled with. I'm, uh, *fiery...peppery...full of fight and show....*"

Marcus laughed aloud. "I think I'll take my chances."

Eleven

⁂

"I sleep, but my heart waketh."
Song of Solomon 5:2, The Holy Bible

Paper or plastic?" Before Marcus could even open his mouth to respond, a laughing voice broke in, "Ah, now that's an environmental dilemma, if I ever heard one!"

Marcus smiled at the woman passing his check-out counter. "Hi, Val. How's it going?"

"Paper or plastic?" The skinny bag boy was becoming impatient.

"Yeah, I can't wait to hear this! Hm…what will the editor of *High Sierra* do?" Standing with a large bag of groceries in her arms, Valerie made a show of watching Marcus very carefully.

He pretended to weigh the issue "I think I'd have to say…paper. No, plastic! No…definitely paper. Paper." The bag boy did not look amused.

"What!" Valerie feigned indignation. "And kill a tree?"

Marcus laughed. "It's okay. I recycle. And anyway, when did you become the Waste Police?" Marcus absently wrote out a check while they spoke.

"Oh, I'm not." A pale hand waved through the air

dismissively. "I just like giving you a hard time. So what have you been up to lately, besides making life miserable for new photographers in town?"

He gave her a look of great surprise. "How did you know about that?"

"Small town. Big ears."

"Seriously." Marcus muttered a quiet thank-you to the clerk and gathered his two bags of groceries. Matching his stride with Valerie's own long legs, Marcus joined her in walking out to the parking lot.

"Seriously. Oh, I met Celia the first day she got into town. She seems great."

"Great," Marcus agreed. "Smart, too. And funny—"

"Beautiful, too," the blonde remarked.

Marcus ignored her. "*And* she's saving our hide over at the office. It's not easy to find someone who will traipse off across the country at a moment's notice like that. She's a dream."

"Oooh? A *dream*, huh?"

"Now, Valerie." Marcus tried to look and sound stern. "Get that glint out of your eye!"

"Who, me?"

"Yeah. Very convincing," Marcus said, looking unconvinced. "I will not play Hodel to your Yente."

"I wouldn't expect you to. Why ever would you think such a thing?" Valerie marched ahead of him across the asphalt, singing under her breath, "Matchmaker, matchmaker, make me a match. Hm, hm, hm, *hm....* "

"You're incorrigible."

"Yeah? Well, you're impossible."

85

Marcus sighed. "Give me a chance. I'll find somebody in my own time," he called after Val's retreating form.

"Whatever. It's your funeral," she threw back over her shoulder. "After all, it's not every day you meet someone who's a 'dream.' "

Beneath the brightly colored, log cabin quilt, Celia wriggled and moaned, fighting the disturbing images that danced across her mind. At her feet, Hank grumbled in complaint, then resettled his small, taut body against the comfort of her legs.

As the pictures in her subconscious began to take shape, Celia found herself back in college taking finals once again. *Almost over. It's almost over.* The sentiment remained unspoken yet permeated every element of her vision. *Almost over.*

Then, before they'd even begun, the tests were through. Celia stood before the university president, wearing cap and gown, holding out a hand to accept the long-coveted diploma. "Mom! Dad!" Her face the perfect picture of the pride of youth, she turned to scan the crowd; the bleachers stood empty.

Suddenly, the campus and crowd of beaming students were gone. Celia found herself, instead, at the edge of a long, rocky precipice. Five hundred feet to her right stood an unidentifiable figure; beyond it waited a second. Further down the cliff, a third.

Instinctively, Celia began to run toward the first figure. Her pulse pounding, she raced faster and faster as feelings of fear and dread crept over her, infecting her entire being. Slowly, the image began to take shape. Strong, wide shoulders, graying temples, olive complexion....

"Father?"

She tried to increase her speed, but her feet felt as if they were caught in quicksand. On and on Celia pushed, desperate to reach the man at the cliff. There was something she had to tell him, something he did not know.

"Father!"

She tried to catch his attention, but he kept looking away to the mountains, to the second figure along the cliff—everywhere but the ledge upon which he stood.

At last Celia began to draw close. Twenty more steps. *I've got to tell him.* Ten. *Almost there.* She stretched out a hand....

But he was gone.

"No!" Celia's cry was one of pure anguish. She stepped to the rocks and peered over. Just beyond the precipice floated a thick layer of murky-gray clouds. It was impossible to determine where he had gone.

"Father?"

Could he still hear her?

Celia sunk to her knees and buried her face in her hands, weeping soundlessly, violently. Despite her uncontrollable shaking, the tears would not come. Peering through her fingers, down the edge of the cliff, Celia could barely make out the second figure. Instinctively, she pulled herself to her feet and began to rush along the rocks once again; this time, the effort was even more of a strain than the last. The stranger's features began to take form. Soft, fine hair, delicate limbs, proudly raised chin...

"Mama?"

Celia threw herself forward as the woman wandered closer to the ledge. "No! Stop!"

The woman stood less than thirty feet away; Celia was sure she must have heard her. But she seemed quite determined, sure of her intentions to step toward the cliff.

"*Mother!*"

It was too late.

Shaking with shock and grief, Celia turned to the next figure.

Paul.

She could hear his laugh even before she could make out his face. With every last bit of energy she could muster, she pushed herself forward. This time it would be different. It had to be different. He was moving toward her. He didn't belong at the cliff. He wasn't anywhere near the edge.

"Hurry up, C! You can't catch me!" With a hearty chuckle, the man turned on his heel and began to run.

"Paul! DON'T!"

The cliff lay abandoned. The last figure was gone.

Throwing herself upon the rocky outcropping, Celia cried into the soupy gray, "Why? Wasn't one enough? What about *me?*"

Strangely, nothing echoed back from the canyon. Not even her own voice.

Suddenly, further down the precipice, another figure appeared—tall, healthy, strong. The man was a stranger, yet seemed somehow familiar. Behind him stood a crowd of faceless people, including a slender blonde whom Celia sensed that she should know. They, too, stood dangerously close to the edge of the cliff. The man reached out one steady, tanned hand.

Celia looked from the slippery rocks before her to the mountains at her back. A line from an old western haunted her. *Head for the hills....* She wiped the dust from her hands and began to retreat.

"Wait...." The stranger took a step forward, but Celia turned away. The ground felt hard and cold beneath her feet. The voice continued to call, "Celia!" He was only steps behind her.

"Don't run! Wait!" His breath was on her neck. He had only to reach out and she would be caught.

"NO!"

Celia woke with a start. The bedclothes were knotted tightly about clammy legs. Hank glared at her accusingly.

Too shaken to even attempt to joke, Celia pulled the sleepy hound into her arms and began to cry softly.

Twelve

❧

"A friend may well be reckoned the masterpiece of Nature."
Ralph Waldo emerson, *Essays*, 'Friendship'

S o, how's my favorite photographer?" Valerie asked, as she sat across from Celia in the booth.

Celia ignored the question, so taken was she with the sight before her—one plate piled high with fresh, mixed greens and a second overflowing with succulent bay scallops topped by bright red and yellow peppers.

"Where did these come from?"

Valerie adopted her most condescending tone. "The *ocean.* See, there are these little things called *mollusks.* Come on. Say it with me... *mol-*lusks. They're part of the animal kingdom, of the phylum—"

"All right! I get the point." Celia laughed. "I'm just surprised. Lundy hardly seems like the seafood capital of the world."

"We're not on Mars, you know," Valerie protested. "It's not like we're out of contact with *all* of civilization."

"It's not?" Celia kept her voice even, baiting.

Valerie rolled her eyes. "Of course not. I'm sure these things came in fresh this morning, right off the mule train."

"Mule train!" Celia snorted in laughter. Valerie shot her friend a disparaging look and clicked thumb and forefinger in front of her eyes.

"Snap out of it. Get serious, girl. I want to know all the dirt. How's the shoot going? Do you like the magazine? What about Marcus—?"

Celia seized upon her last question. "Oh! Marcus! That man is impossible." She proceeded to bring Valerie up to date, in great detail, regarding Marcus's exploits. As she talked, she waved her arms animatedly and her voice rose in pitch and intensity. Soon she was perched on the edge of her seat, appearing to be in danger of falling off with her next enthusiastic gesture.

"…and then he started comparing me to a mangy little rodent.…"

" 'Rodent'?"

"Some sort of crummy squirrel."

"Aw. Squirrels are cute."

Celia blushed. "Cute? *Cute?* He didn't say I had the grace of a gazelle or the voice of a dove. He didn't say I had the eyes of a doe or the bearing of a lioness. He said I was prickly and dreadful, and full of fight…or some such horrible thing."

"Why would he say that?"

"Oh, I don't know. Maybe because.…"

" 'Because'?"

Celia sounded petulant. "Okay! Maybe because I *was* prickly and dreadful, and full of fight."

" '…or some such horrible thing,'" Valerie finished for her.

"Yeah." Celia sat sullen and quiet.

"You sound disappointed about the whole affair."

"*Disappointed? Affair?* Oh, now there's a laugh! The only thing disappointing about it is that I didn't punch him in the nose for being such a *jerk*."

" '*The lady doth protest too much, methinks.*'"

"Oh, yeah? The lady doth *butt in* too much, methinks."

Valerie waved her napkin in the air in a signal of surrender. "Okay, okay. I'm only trying to help. I just think it's pretty interesting, the way you got yourself all worked up like that the minute his name came up."

When Celia didn't answer, Valerie reached across the table and squeezed her hand. "What if you *did* like him? Now, I'm not saying that you do," she amended, as Celia opened her mouth to argue. "I'm just saying, 'What if?' What would be so bad about that?"

"There wouldn't be any point," Celia managed, reluctantly.

"What do you mean?"

"I mean, I'm happy the way things are. I don't need some man in my life, messing things up. It isn't worth the hassle."

"Hassle?"

"That's right. *Hassle.* I'm not about to get all worked up over somebody who isn't right for me anyway."

Valerie looked at her in surprise. "Well, that's certainly a defeatist attitude."

"Not defeatist," Celia insisted. "Realistic. Every one of my school friends has grown up and found the person she wanted to spend the rest of her life with. I'm twenty-nine years old. I think if it was going to happen, it would have happened by now."

"That's ridiculous!" Valerie protested. "I'm only thirty-four, and I haven't given up hope. We're just babies!" She made an odd face. "And thank you *very much* for making me feel so secure about my chances."

"Sorry," Celia flashed her a weak smile of apology. "I used to have hope, too. I had this whole fairy-tale mentality. I was sure that one day the man of my dreams would come riding into my life, and when he did, he'd take one good look at me and be so stricken by love, he'd fall right off that white horse at my feet."

"You're a very strange girl," Valerie said, keeping her face straight.

Celia gave her an amused glance and continued. "In my dream, once he fell off that horse, I saw that he was really just a man and not a prince at all. He'd just *looked* like a prince from a distance. But that was okay with me. After all, I was just a peasant girl myself. And the thing that was so wonderful about him was that he knew that about me, but he treated me like a princess just the same." For a moment she felt almost peaceful.

"That's a beautiful story. Maybe the fairy tale will come true?"

The almost-peaceful feeling had left, and Celia felt emotionless once again. "Not for me."

"Why not?" Valerie looked concerned.

"Because I *did* meet that prince…the man of my dreams. And he didn't exactly fall off the horse."

Valerie looked at Celia's grim face. "I gather he didn't treat you like a princess either?"

"Oh, he did for awhile. And then he rode away again."

"I see."

Celia sighed. "I wish *I* did. That's the hard part. Not knowing why he left. I keep turning it over and over in my head, trying to figure out what was wrong with me. I wasn't pretty enough, wasn't exciting enough, wasn't strong enough. At the time, I was struggling, trying to understand…to keep things together. And then the next thing I knew, he was gone. I mean, *really* gone." She stared off into the distance. "It was the first rain after a three-month dry spell. You know how the roads get extra slick when the water hits all that built-up oil? They think that's what happened. Paul was in a rush, probably not paying attention to the roads. He died before the first rescue truck even reached the scene." Celia touched shaking hands to her flushed face. "I never got a chance to say good-bye, to tell him I was sorry. We'd just had this horrible fight—" Her voice broke.

"Oh, Cel—it wasn't your fault."

"But it *was*. I made it happen."

"How can you make such a thing happen?"

"I wanted too much. And then I got what was coming to me."

"You make it sound like you were being punished."

Celia did not answer.

"Is that it? You think—what? That God is punishing you? Why?"

Celia shrugged.

"No, come on, answer me," Valerie insisted. "What could you possibly have done that would be so horrible?"

"I don't know!" Celia's voice rose to a wail. "I wish I did, but I don't. All I know is he's taken away everyone I love. My dad, my mom…Paul. Things like that don't just happen! There must be a reason. God wouldn't have let it happen if he loved me."

"I don't know if that's true, but at least you still believe he exists."

"Well…yeah," Celia admitted. "I just try not to think about it."

"Why?"

"Because, even if he does, it doesn't matter. He doesn't love me."

"You don't believe in a God of love?"

Celia was quiet for a moment. "That's not what I said. I said he doesn't love *me*."

Valerie's eyes filled with compassion. "Oh, Celia! What would make you say such a thing?"

"Because it's true. I'm not a shallow person, Val. I love being successful at my job…I like nice things. But ultimately, I've never been all that excited about money or power or fame. I loved my *family*. My parents and I weren't all that close when I was growing up. But I really did love them. They were all I had. When my dad passed away, I thought part of me died, too. We never talked all that much. And affection wasn't a real big thing in our house. I was just a kid. I didn't know how to show it. I don't know if he ever knew how much I loved him." Celia picked at her salad. "After he was gone, at least I still had my mom. I knew she needed me, and I had my love for her to keep me going. But then, before I was grown up—before I was able to shoulder adult responsibilities, take care of her, show her what she meant to me—she was gone, too. I wasn't…bitter, exactly, although I think I was starting to toughen up. I didn't want anyone to take care of me. I was moving forward, living my life. And then Paul came along. I wasn't looking for him—for anyone—but there he was, full of life and laughter. You know that old legend, the one about a single soul being separated and put into the bodies of two babies, and how those two spend a lifetime trying to find one another again? I know it's just a story, but that's how it felt to be with Paul. Like I'd found my other half...."

"Oh, honey...." Valerie reached across the table.

"No!" Celia pushed the comforting hand away. "You think there's a God, don't you? That's why you said what you did about believing he exists. Well, maybe you're right. Maybe he *is* out there somewhere. But I don't want to play his games."

" 'Games'?"

"I was perfectly fine, minding my own business, when He plopped Paul down in the middle of my life, like a big, old carrot. But then, every time I took a step forward, he'd pull on the string and drag Paul further away."

"Celia, that wasn't God. That was Paul. He wasn't a puppet, you know."

"Why didn't God tell him I was the one?"

"I'm not so sure that's God's job. We all have free choice."

"Didn't God know I'd be hurt if he let Paul be a part of my life?"

"Yeah," Valerie conceded. "He knew."

"Then why did he do it? Why didn't he help me? I prayed. If he had to send someone, why didn't he send me someone who would love me?"

"Celia," Valerie spoke carefully. "You didn't need anyone else to love you. God did. He *does.* That's enough. You matter to *him.*"

"I still don't get it."

"Well...." Valerie thought for a moment. "I guess it's sort of the way it is with you and Hank."

"*Hank?*"

"Let's say you were to tell Hank he can't have that piece of pizza, because…. Oh, bad example. Let's try again. Say you have fried chicken for dinner, and Hank is making you feel guilty. You want to make him happy, but you know those scraps could kill him. So you say, 'Sorry, Hank. You can't have those bones. They're bad for you.' Would it be his fault that he didn't understand you? Of course not! Now, I know you guys communicate pretty well. But he's a *dog,* after all. He's not going to understand the 'why.' He only hears the 'No.' That's like us—no matter how we try, we won't understand 'why' every time God says 'No.' We just have to trust that he knows what's best. I can't tell you why he allowed what he did in your life. I *can* tell you that he knows you are hurting, and he cares. But anything he allows, he allows for a reason."

Celia's eyes began to tear up; she felt thoroughly miserable.

"These are real issues," Valerie assured her. "And it's good to talk about them. You have to work them through. Ask yourself the tough questions. Does God really exist? If he does, can I trust him? If you find that you *must* be able to trust him, then you need to do it. Do some reading. Find out what he says. There are some powerful promises in the Scriptures. The one that helps me most is Jeremiah 29:11: "'For I know the plans I have for you,' declares the LORD, 'plans to prosper you, and not to harm you, plans to give you hope and a future.' He doesn't want to harm you, no matter what you believe. It won't help you to believe that he's out to get you; it's bound to make you paranoid. Celia, you've got to know that he loves you. If he doesn't—," Valerie spoke carefully. "Then who have you got?"

Celia's eyes brimmed with tears.

"Don't get me wrong—I'm here for you," the slender blonde assured her. "I want to be your friend. But I'm only human, after all. There's only so much I can do, so much I can be for you. The rest has to come from within." She pointed at her heart. "And from above. The rest of that verse says, ' "Then you will call upon Me and come and pray to Me, and I will listen to you. You will seek Me and find Me when you seek Me with all your heart. *I will be found by you,* " declares the LORD.' "

Celia stared at the soggy mess on her plate. "Gee. You sure know how to ruin a nice lunch." She forced a lightness into her tone. "I think I've over-salted my scallops."

"Sorry." Valerie smiled apologetically. "I just care more about your heart than your stomach. Are you okay?"

"Yeah, I'm okay." Celia dabbed at her face with a linen napkin and managed a tiny smile. "What do you say we ditch this joint and grab a burger?" She looked around nervously, wanting nothing more than to escape the restaurant before anyone saw the state she was in.

"It's a deal." Valerie signaled that they were ready to pay.

Celia sighed as she held a glass of ice water to her burning cheeks. "I bet I look all puffed up like a chipmunk."

Valerie gave her an impish grin. "Better that than a 'crummy squirrel.' "

CHAPTER

Thirteen

❧

*"This creature man, who in his own selfish affairs is
a coward to the backbone, will fight for an idea like a hero.*
George Bernard Shaw, *Man and Superman*

Knock, knock." Celia peered into Rob's office, the site of her humiliating initiation to *High Sierra*. "Anybody home?" Rob raised his shaggy blonde head from the art table and beamed. "So you decided to come back! I was afraid we might have scared you away from the office for good."

"Don't be silly," Celia scolded, sounding more confident than she felt. "I can take a joke," she assured him, as she stepped into the room.

"I'm sure you can," Rob agreed amicably. His eyes settled on her camera bag. "So, what have you brought me?"

"Shots of the Knapps' place." Celia reached into her pouch for the canisters. "Did Marcus give you the film from my first shoot?"

"Sure did."

"Have you gotten anything back yet?"

"You bet." Rob pulled a stack of transparencies from one drawer. "And there are some real beauts in here."

"Great! That's what I wanted to hear." Celia moved to stand beside him. Soon the two were hunched over Rob's light table, absorbed in a discussion about the upcoming article and the subjects Celia still needed to shoot. Twenty minutes later, sitting side by side at the desk, they were comparing Rob's rough design to an article from the April 1993 issue when Marcus walked into the room and cleared his throat.

"*Excuse me,* please." Somehow, he managed to make those three simple words sound sarcastic. "I realize you two are terribly busy. But if you don't mind, Celia, I'd like you to stop by my office and bring me up to speed on how things are going. That is, whenever you and Rob finish your little art review." He stalked out of the room without waiting for either one to respond.

Celia stared after him, openmouthed. "*What* is that man's problem? Just when I begin to think he might be a decent guy—"

Rob looked positively gleeful. "Well, I'll be…. Marcus is finally getting tormented by the little green monster!"

"Wha—? Jealousy? What's he got to be jealous about?"

"Are you kidding? You and me, of course! Here we are, sitting close together at my desk, looking all cozy—"

Celia lowered her head and looked down her nose. "Rob, don't be alarmed, but I think you may be losing your marbles."

The art director laughed. "I don't think so. You haven't been around him all week like I have. Every day it's Celia Randall this, and Celia Randall that. Frankly, I'm sick of hearing your name—no offense intended."

"None taken."

Rob looked thoughtful. "I thought his behavior seemed a little strange, but now it all makes sense!"

Celia shook her head. "If you ask me, he's just a moody guy. Besides, you're acting like I'm the only woman he's ever spoken to. The way I hear it, he's a regular Don Juan."

Rob made a face. "Who, Marcus? *Our* Marcus? Marcus *Stratton?*"

"Well…yeah." Celia was confused by his reaction. "It sounds like the women around here just love him."

"Oh, that." Rob nodded. "Well, they do. That's true. And he's nice to them, all right. But he's certainly no Don Juan. He usually hangs out with me and a couple of the other guys in town. Every month or two, he gets a visit from one of his college friends or someone in his family. But for the most part, he just works. A man's got only so much energy, and Marcus puts all his into protecting the mountains he loves."

"Until now," Celia mumbled thoughtfully.

"What's that?"

"Well, it seems like all of a sudden he's putting all this emphasis on being trendy. If protecting the Sierra is so important to him, then why is he giving up so easily?"

"Well, now, you have to realize that it isn't as simple as all that. Things have been rough around here for the past few months. There's a lot of pressure on Marcus. A new competitor is moving in, and his company has got the financial backing—and the contacts—to send complimentary copies to readers on a few of the bigger magazines' mailing lists. Naturally, some of our advertisers are threatening to defect, at least during that introductory period. Chances are, though, once they go, they're gone for good. Marcus has fought for months now to keep their support, but it just keeps looking worse and worse. Some days I get the feeling he's about ready to cave."

"You're taking it all pretty calmly. I guess you don't mind the changes?"

The man's characteristically sunny face clouded over. "I wouldn't say that. Marcus knows where I stand, and we've had some pretty intense discussions about it. But it's easy for me to stay starry-eyed. Marcus is the one with all the pressure." Rob looked increasingly uncomfortable. "The thing is, Marcus really is one of the truly honorable men in this world. I hate it when good doesn't triumph over evil. I want Marcus to keep fighting—to be a hero. But maybe ten years is enough for any man."

"Maybe." Celia felt a trace of sadness creeping into her own heart. "A person can only take so much stress and pain. And after all, what they say is true—every man has his breaking point."

Fourteen

❧

"Let us go then, you and I, When the evening is spread out against the sky."
T.S. Eliot, 'Love Song of J. Alfred Prufrock'

Hey, Douglas! How's it going?" Celia slipped the plastic cap back onto her lens with a snap. "Awful! How am I supposed to get any decent shots of the duck pond when there aren't any stinking ducks? What am I supposed to do, say, 'Here's the pond' and draw them in?"

Marcus walked toward her, clucking sympathetically, arms folded across his broad chest. "What'd you do? Scare them all away?"

"I don't know!" Celia's cry bordered on a wail. "They were all over the place the other day. Now it's like they've gone into hiding or something. I think it's a conspiracy."

Marcus surveyed the darkening sky. "Could be they know something we don't. Maybe they decided to take cover."

"Wimps!" Celia pouted. "So there are a few clouds. Big deal. Like birds never get *wet?*"

Marcus chuckled again. "Sorry. I know it's been hard to get the shots you need. What rotten timing! It was gorgeous all

103

summer…until *you* came along."

The petite brunette held up a hand as if holding him at bay. "I'm warning you, mister…don't pick a fight with me today." Her eyes narrowed. "I'm liable to rip your head off and eat you for lunch."

"Whoa! Thanks for the warning. Actually…" He turned away, casually. "I was wondering if you might want to take a little break this afternoon. You've been working ever since you got here. It's time you got a feel for the real Sierra. Maybe we could grab a bite, go for a drive…I could show you around the area a bit before it gets too dark."

Celia felt her pulse strangely quicken. "Take off early, huh? What am I supposed to tell my boss? I've got a hot date?" *Ohhh. Please…somebody rip out my tongue. Why did I stop there? Why not just propose, for crying out loud?* Celia suddenly pretended to be very interested in the plastic film canister clutched in her palm.

"A 'hot date', huh? Oh, I don't know.…" Marcus's voice was unusually soft. "That guy's such a dud…I'm not so sure he'd understand. I bet he hasn't been on a real date in, oh…months. Maybe years."

"Oh, come on!" Celia forgot about the film canister. "I'm supposed to believe that?"

"Believe whatever you want," Marcus threw over his shoulder as he strode away. "But be ready in an hour. Dress casual. I'll pick you up at your house at four-thirty sharp." He sauntered back to the car, whistling loudly, and in two different keys.

Celia watched as the dust from the Land Cruiser whirled, then settled; the sight held her gaze even after the vehicle was gone.

Now what?

There was nothing to do but pack up her things and head back to the house. Pulling her equipment together haphazardly, Celia found herself completely consumed by feelings of excitement and apprehension. So focused was her concentration, that all other thoughts—including those regarding the offensive ducks—were pushed from her mind.

Celia carefully studied the selection before her. Coral flowered sun dress—*too cutesy. You'll look like Thumbelina.* White pinpoint oxford with denim skirt—*too short. Makes you look like you have sausages for legs.* Worn, cut-off shorts, frayed along the hem—*yeah, right. Hi, I'm a slob…where are we going for dinner?*

After ten minutes of deliberation, Celia finally selected a graceful taupe sarong and white, short-sleeved, rib-knit top. Tiny pearls dangled from her ear lobes and macramé espadrilles covered slim, tanned feet. Celia reached for a vial of perfume and paused with her arm in mid-air, considering her reflection.

What difference does it make what I look…or smell like? He's my boss. My boss! Still…. Celia gave in to her instincts and seized the tiny glass container. *After all, Valerie made me promise to 'play nice'.*

Marcus arrived at four-thirty on the button. Dressed in wheat-colored chinos and khaki-striped seersucker shirt, he emanated both comfort and confidence.

Gazing upon Celia as she greeted him at the door, he made no effort to hide his admiration. "Douglas!" His tone was light. "You look…incredible."

Celia waved him indoors, then hid her shaking hands behind her back. "Come in. And, please, there's no need to be formal…call me 'Doug'. "

Marcus grinned. *We do seem to match wits perfectly,* Celia thought.

"All right, Douggie. Are you ready? You might want to grab a coat. It might be chilly later. Those clouds are still coming in."

Celia grabbed a chestnut-colored suede jacket and called toward the living room, "Hank?" She turned back to Marcus. "I can put him outside, but would you mind terribly if he came with us? He's been cooped up all week. I'm afraid if I leave him behind one more time, he'll petition to become an emancipated canine."

Marcus looked slightly doubtful. "What'll he do while we're eating?"

"Oh, probably just roll around in the cab of the Cruiser, leaving dog hair everywhere. Then he might rub his nose all over the windows, leaving little, runny marks, like snail tracks. He might even bark at all the people walking by, getting really, really wound up, so that when we come back he's bloodthirsty and ready to attack."

"Ha. Ha. I was serious."

"And I wasn't?"

"Really."

"Okay…really. We're going someplace casual, right? Is there a place with a covered porch? We'll just take his leash and peg him outside."

Marcus shrugged his shoulders. "Sounds reasonable."

Hank ambled into the kitchen and raised his hairy head, looking from one figure to the other. His bloodshot gaze finally rested upon Marcus.

"What's he staring at?"

"I think he wants to know what your intentions are."

"Ah." Marcus looked the animal square in the eye. "I intend to take your mom, here, and go get something nice to eat. Maybe a hot *dog*, or a corn *dog*...."

"How rude!"

"Aw...I'll give him some leftovers later. I have a feeling he can be bought."

Celia watched as Marcus took the leash from the door handle and hooked it to the collar around Hank's neck. *"I intend to take your mom, here...."* He understood her relationship with Hank. How sweet.

She squelched the happy feeling. "Yeah...well. Just don't call him *Frank* ever again."

Uncomfortable with meeting Marcus's intense gaze, Celia averted her eyes and surveyed her surroundings. The Madre (named in honor of "the other Sierra") was dimly lit, making it difficult to fully appreciate the exposed brick and stained pine walls, or to closely observe the other dozen or so customers. From corner speakers blared an eclectic sampling of recordings: Irish folk, smooth jazz, R & B. One solitary, harried waiter scurried from table to table, a wooden smile plastered upon his face.

Celia poked at the immense sesame chicken salad the waiter had brought her a moment before.

Marcus remained silent. "I make you uncomfortable," he said finally. "Why?"

A tiny seed slipped down Celia's windpipe, causing her to cough violently. "What?" she choked out, as tears rose to her eyes. "Where'd that come from?"

"You've looked like you were in pain for the last thirty minutes. Now you appear to be hunting for an escape route."

"Sorry." The feeling was genuine. Celia cleared her voice and wiped the tears from her eyes. "I—I don't mean to come across like such a stiff…"

"'Stiff?'" Marcus laughed. "*You,* my dear, are anything but stiff. You're terrific—," Celia sniffled and looked doubtful. "—but I hate to think that being with me is such an ordeal for you."

Celia deliberated. *How much do I say?* Despite the fact that she'd wanted to hate him, the time she'd spent with Marcus so far had been surprisingly enjoyable. He was intelligent and well read…she loved their banter. She hadn't laughed so much in over a year. Not since before.… "Oh, Marcus—" She sighed as she spoke his name. "It's not that I'm uncomfortable with you. I'm…uncomfortable with me."

Marcus shook his head. "I don't understand."

"I'm not antisocial. I like people. I like *you,* when you get right down to it. But that's about all I can feel. I don't like getting too attached to people."

"I haven't given you any pressure. This is just dinner—"

"I know, I know. And I don't mean to imply that it's anything else. I just—I'll only be here a couple more weeks. I don't really want us to become best pals or anything. Pretty soon, I'll be gone. I don't want to miss anyone. Who needs that?"

"So…what are you going to do? Choose some place to settle down, find a nice guy, start a little family?"

"No. I'm going to travel more. In the last year, I've gotten really serious about my work. I can't stay in one place any longer. It wouldn't be good for me, artistically."

"Then you plan to keep running from town to town, never connecting with anyone?"

"Weeell…you don't have to make it sound like that." Celia traced a finger around the rim of her water glass.

"But that's what you're saying. Right?"

"Yes, that's right. You're right…YOU'RE RIGHT…*YOU'RE RIGHT!* Okay? I said it. Are you happy?"

Marcus slammed his coffee cup down on the varnished surface. "No, I am not happy. I feel awful for you."

Celia began to feel more and more like a prickly squirrel. "I don't need your pity…."

"It's not pity." Marcus seemed to make an effort to sound patient. "It's *concern.* Celia…people *like* you. You're an extremely likable woman."

"Not *that* likable."

"Why would you say that?"

"Because if I was *really* likable…oh, never mind."

"What?"

"For*get* it." Her voice held a hint of warning. "It's history."

Marcus looked ready to explode. "It's not history. It's right here, right now…whatever it is. It's affecting you and your ability to love."

"Love! Where'd that come from?"

"Love…like…whatever." Marcus backpedaled. "Don't change the subject."

"*What* subject?"

"I don't know! You. Me. Our friendship."

"Honestly, Marcus. We barely know each other! Why is this even an issue?"

Marcus held her eyes with his own. "Because I care about you." His voice rumbled, deep and soft. "This matters. *You* matter."

You matter.

Celia sucked in her breath. Where had she heard those words recently? When was the last time someone had told her she mattered? Was it Paul? Surely it was Paul. What was it he had said? *You're incredible.* He'd stood beside her at the first major showing of her work, drawn to the beauty of each piece, stirred by the symbolism. *I knew you had talent. You'll be famous some day.* He couldn't have been more supportive. So why had it felt so shallow?

You matter.

Suddenly, an image danced across her mind—her mother rushing about the house, overly dramatizing her fear that she would arrive late to yet another meeting. She gave her child a benevolent glance. *Did you finish your homework, Celia? That's wonderful! You're Mama's good little girl, aren't you?* A later memory followed, a scene from after Celia's father's funeral—her mother, now subdued, withdrawn, unreachable. She had remained that way for several years, until her own death from a major stroke.

You matter.

Celia tried to remember if her father had ever said such a thing. Memories of him were faint. Clearer was the image of his empty chair. *Mama, tell Daddy I said goodnight.*

You matter.

"Celia?"

She forced her attention back to the man who looked at her with such concern. Something inside her fought against her natural instincts to pull back.

She took a deep breath. "My parents died when I was barely more than a kid. For two years I dated a man who suddenly decided he didn't want to get married. I don't feel like getting attached to anyone anymore. And you just seem awfully—," Celia paused. *Be honest.* "—easy to get attached to." She felt herself blushing.

Marcus seemed unshaken by her confession. "So what we're dealing with here is the basic animal response to conflict—fight or flee?"

"I…guess so." Celia shifted uncomfortably.

Marcus reached across the table and touched her fingers gently. "I don't mind the fight. Actually, I kind of like it. Just don't flee. Okay?"

Her green eyes glistened like emeralds. Celia nodded, unable to speak.

"Well, then…." Marcus snapped his fingers in the direction of the wooden man. "Garçon? Garçon?" He grinned at Celia mischievously. "Okay, squirrel…what'll it be for dessert? Pecan pie? Almond tart? *Nut* bread?"

Fifteen

❧

"The sea! The sea!"
Xenophon, Anabasis

W here are you taking me?"

"The *'dead sea of California…a lifeless, treeless, hideous desert.'*"

"Yuk." Celia covered her ears. "That sounds awful. Muir again?"

"*Un*-unh. Mark Twain."

"Twain? When was he ever in the Sierra?" Celia glanced outside at the passing thickets—bright buffalo berry, sweetbrier, flowering willow.

"Are you kidding?" Marcus feigned shock. "Where'd you go to school? Twain *loved* the West. It was right around the mid-1800s."

"All right, Trivia King. So what's the name of this 'hideous' place?"

"Mono Lake."

"Wha—?" Celia shook her head thoughtfully. "That's so strange. The name sounds familiar, like I should— Oh! The lake in the article. One of your first issues, right? 'Paradise Lost'…Mono Lake."

"Ouch!" Marcus winced at her pronunciation. "Not like mononucleosis, Celia. It's *Moh*-noh. As in, 'Oh, no.'"

"All right, *Moh*-noh. But if *Moh*-noh is such a wasteland, then why are we going there, of all places?"

"Ah…that's the mystery, isn't it?" Marcus looked quite pleased with himself. "I guess you'll just have to wait and see."

"I feel like an idiot!" Despite her protests, Celia smiled broadly as she tugged at the bandanna over her eyes.

"Hey! No cheating." Marcus's fingers were warm around hers. "Just a few more steps. I want you to get the impact all at once."

Celia sniffed the air delicately. "What's that smell?"

"Smell?"

"It's sort of like…the ocean."

"The ocean! Don't be ridiculous! We're miles from any ocean."

"Well, *duh*."

"Hey, now! Careful…" Marcus jostled her arm. "You're at my mercy." He stopped for a moment. "Yo, Hank! Get the lead out." Branches rustled to their right, and the hound trotted out cheerfully from behind a clump of coyote brush. "You sure you don't want him on a leash?"

"No, he's fine. Where's he going to go? Besides, Hank thinks that thing is some kind of evil— Whoops!" Celia struggled to regain her balance as she slipped on a pile of loose stones. "Are we almost there?"

"We…ARE…THERE!" Marcus removed the handkerchief

from her eyes with a flourish. "Ta-*da!*"

Celia stood as if frozen. Before her, licking at her feet, was an enormous body of deep azure water. To the left, one island of charcoal-colored sediment lay exposed from the lake; at its right, loomed an immense expanse of white sand. Along Mono's shoreline, and rising from the water, towered hundreds of eerie-looking, white stone columns.

The entire scene was striking, but it was the odd, grayish tufa that held her attention. At a height of ten to thirty feet each, they loomed overhead like shafts of moon rock, or knobby minarets of a substance resembling petrified cauliflower. For one wild moment, Celia almost believed she was no longer in the Sierra but in some previously unexplored land with inhabitants unknown. She shivered.

"—and that's Black Point," Marcus was saying. "The small island, there, is Negit. She was formed by the eruption of a dark cinder cone. The lighter one is Paoha, her sister."

Celia remained speechless. Her eyes traveled along the horizon, drinking in the snowy white mountains and gray volcanic peaks of the Mono craters.

"Put your hand in the water," Marcus suggested. "Feel it."

Celia knelt and did as she was told. Surprisingly, the liquid felt quite slick, almost slimy. "Ow!" She stuck her fingers in her mouth to relieve the sting to two small paper cuts she'd received the day before. "Hey! This is bitter!"

"That's right," Marcus nodded. "You're at one of our country's only inland seas. It's almost three times as salty as the ocean."

"But—I don't get it. Why is this lake different from all the others?"

"It has to do with the level of dissolved carbonates, sulfates—"

"Uh…in English, please, Mr. Science?"

Marcus raised his eyebrows. "There are five waterways that feed *into* Mono, but none that pour out. When the streams flow into the lake, they bring all sorts of salts and minerals they've collected from rocks and soil along the way. When the water evaporates, it leaves all the other gunk behind."

" 'Gunk. *Gunk?*' Is that a technical term?"

"Smart aleck." He gently bumped against her shoulder, like a bashful schoolboy. "You wanted the A-B-C version."

Celia peered into the saline water. "How can anything *live* in there?"

"Well, most things don't. Fish can't handle it. There isn't much in there but these tiny, wormy-looking brine shrimp, and billions of alkali flies."

"Gross." Celia put her face close to the lake's briny surface and watched as the thread-like creatures swept through the water, filtering algae into their mouths for nourishment.

"Yeah, well…they're an important part of the food chain. Just about every kind of North American shorebird comes here to feed and raise their young. We see California gulls, Wilson's phalaropes, snowy plovers—"

"Look!" Celia pointed as across the sky a gray and white gull swooped overhead, arching its wings gracefully, then diving at the brine-filled waters. Several of the bird's companions followed their leader, swooping past the ominous limestone columns. Celia gazed in wonder at the haunting spires. "Where'd those things *come* from?"

"Underground springs rich in calcium used to bubble

beneath these waters, creating the tufa. The waves worked and shaped them. After the lake receded, the spires could be seen above the new water line."

"They're like…sculptures. Wonderful works of art." Celia held her breath reverently. Marcus stood at her elbow, watching silently with her. He was close enough that she could smell his sweet, musky cologne. *Close enough to reach out and touch….*

"Hey! What's it like to swim in there?" Celia moved away, her voice forced and bright.

"Well, you felt what the water did to your hand. The alkali can sting a little. But, for the most part, it's very nice. And you float like a cork! I wouldn't let Hank try it, though." He turned in the direction of a nearby shrub, from which the hound dog's tag and collar could be heard jangling.

"Why not?" Celia glanced toward the animal protectively.

"Oh…now, how did Twain put it? After he brought his own dog here, he wrote something like…. *'We had…the rawest dog I almost ever saw. He jumped overboard…the alkali nipped him in all the raw places…and by the time he got to shore there was no bark to him—for he had barked the bark all out of his inside, and the water had cleaned the bark all of his outside, and he probably wished he had never embarked in any such enterprise.'"*

Celia's expression was blank. "You," she said dryly, "have a mind like a steel trap."

Marcus nodded proudly.

"I wonder—" Celia peered into his ear. "—what other bits of useless information you have stored in there?"

"All kinds," he agreed cheerfully.

Her eyes danced with silent laughter. "Heaven help us."

Marcus turned away, his expression more solemn. "Sometimes I think the lake's going to need heaven's help."

"Oh...yeah. The article. What happened, exactly?"

"Back in the forties, some of the water and power guys from L.A. determined that the area was too barren to farm and too cold to live in, and so they figured they'd divert the water to where it would serve a greater number of people. Around the time of the Owens Valley grab, they dug a 12-mile tunnel under the Mono craters, and redirected the water to the city, 350 miles south. The problem is, even though Mono has no outlets, the water began to evaporate at a greater rate than it was feeding in, and the lake started to dry up." Marcus pointed to the circle around the lake basin. "Look at those white alkali marks. Like rings around a tub. That's how much the water level has sunk since then. *Forty-five vertical feet.*"

Celia looked unconcerned. "Why is it such a big deal? The lake's still here."

"Ah." Marcus nodded benevolently, like a teacher explaining a difficult concept to a favorite pupil. "But the only reason it's still around is because people have fought for years to save it. If the water level had kept sinking at the rate it was going, there would have been no hope. Not many people were even aware of the problem. And a lot of the people who knew didn't care."

"How could they not care?" Celia turned her trained photographer's eye on the landscape. "It's *gorgeous.*"

"True," Marcus agreed. "Although it's too stark for some. Still, beauty isn't the only issue here. You see Negit over there?" He pointed to the small cinder island. "That's where the gulls go to raise their young. They come because of the brine shrimp, and the safety of the islands. But when the water level slips too low, a land bridge forms to Negit. The coyotes just trot on out, rout the mama birds, and gobble up their eggs and chicks.

"That's horrible!"

"I'm sure the gulls would agree with you. They need those islands to survive. Mono is a key stop on the migratory route. There aren't a lot of alternatives. Many of the other major wetlands on the Pacific's interior flyway have already disappeared. There's a lot at stake." Marcus looked grave.

"I read your article from the eighties." Celia could see this issue was close to his heart. She rested one hand on the soft cotton of his sleeve. "How do things stand now?"

"Well…." Marcus sighed. "Researchers are keeping a close eye on the salt levels. Salinity has doubled since the water diversions first began. If it gets out of hand, the whole ecosystem could get out of balance. If the shrimp were to die off, many of the birds would, too. And then there's the issue of alkali smog."

"Smog? What are you talking about? The skies here are beautiful!"

"Alkali smog is something unique. High winds can kick up pretty fast in the basin. When the lake is at its lowest levels, the dust gets swept off the exposed lake bottom and carried up to one hundred miles away—as far as San Bernardino or Riverside. It can be pretty hard on some folks, especially those with respiratory problems. The dust is so tiny our noses can't filter it out. It goes straight into our lungs."

Celia coughed unconsciously, then blushed at her reaction. "So what's happening now?"

Marcus scratched his stubbled chin thoughtfully. "Oh…there are still a lot of issues being decided. Legislation was passed to keep the water levels from being lowered further, but it isn't a real clear-cut victory. Mainly, it's important that the public remain informed and aware."

"And that's where you come in." Green eyes stared at him intently, daring him to disagree.

"What?"

"Well, that's what you do at the magazine, isn't it? Your promise to Pops...."

"Now, Celia. Don't start...."

"What's the big deal? It's what you do best, isn't it?"

"I won't be doing *any*thing if the magazine goes down. Come on, let's not argue."

"You said you like to fight with me." She gave him an impish grin.

"That's true." Marcus reached out and touched her cheek with gentle fingers. "But I think there's something else I'd like to do more."

"Oh?" Celia's voice was little more than a breath. "There is?"

"There is." Marcus held her eyes firmly with his own. Celia's pulse quickened, and the sound of her pounding heart echoed in her ears as he drew near. Her eyes slipped to the hard line of his jaw, the crazy curve of his lips, the mischievous glint in his eyes...

"Tickle fight!"

"Wha—? NO!" Celia tried to pull away, but he was already too close. Within seconds he had slung her small frame over his shoulders and begun his torment.

"Hank! Help!" Celia screamed. The animal glanced over one furry shoulder, but apparently deciding that she was in no immediate danger, he quickly returned his dirt-covered nose to the burrow he was uncovering.

Marcus gleefully prodded Celia in the ribs as she tried, unsuccessfully, to wriggle free of his hold. "Yell all you want. No one can hear your cries! Ha-ha-ha!" He mimicked an evil laugh. Back and forth he staggered across the rocky shores, threatening to plunge her into the buoyant waters. Celia was strong and full of fight but no match for Marcus's disciplined strength and powerful grip.

After several minutes marked by shrill screams and hysterical laughter, Celia finally gasped out, "I surrender...I surrender! Hank, *save yourself!*"

With a look of great satisfaction, Marcus set Celia firmly back on her feet. "*Surrender.* What a beautiful word. Doesn't it just trip over the tongue? *Surrender.*" He practiced alternate pronunciations. "Sur-*ren*-der. Sur-ren-*der.*"

"Yeah...well, I've got a few more choice words for you, bub. How about 'dead meat?' How about 'better sleep with the light on'? How about...."

"Tsk, tsk. No one likes a poor sport, Dougie." Marcus hooked thumbs in his belt loops and nodded, adopting the stance of Proud but Gracious Winner. "Tell you what. Why don't we head back to Lundy for a cup of java? I'll let you buy, and we'll call it even."

"Weeell." Celia considered his smug expression. "You're just lucky I happen to love coffee. Besides, I forgive you. This evening's too beautiful to stay angry." She threw her arms up into the air as if embracing the mountains and inhaled deeply, skipping several steps ahead. Looking back as she danced, she visually gauged her small lead, then began to sprint.

"Hey! Come back here, you little cheater!" Despite the indignation in his voice, Marcus waited several seconds before running after his prey.

Sixteen

❧

"The bright face of danger."
Robert Louis Stevenson, *Across the Plains,* 'The Lantern-Bearers'

The Land Cruiser rumbled on through the blue-shadowed night, its passengers silent yet peaceful, the spell of inflated self-consciousness broken.

Celia gazed through the glass, spellbound by the dark silhouettes rushing past. Without warning, she reached forward, grabbed a handle, and cranked hard, letting in a rush of icy air. Despite the chill, she held her face against the blast, feeling the wind numb her cheeks, smelling the tangy, sweet/sharp mingling of cedar and pine. "Wonderful," she murmured. "No wonder you love them like you do."

"What's that?"

"The trees, the mountains…everything in this incredible place! Life has more *meaning* out here. Away from the parties and the schmoozing, the materialism and the routine. You have something here that most of us have lost, something simple and pure."

Marcus seemed to consider her comment. "My life here does have meaning," he agreed, after some thought. "I love these mountains. But they aren't the thing that keeps me going."

"Well, then, what *does* keep you going?"

"I'd have to say my faith."

"Hunh." Celia plucked at a loose thread on her skirt. "I would have pegged you as an animist for sure, you're so drawn to nature."

"Oh, no…I don't go that far. I *do* love nature. But I don't think of trees, or rocks, or water as more important than—or even equal to—humans."

"Well, you sure got all fired up about that Owens Valley water grab."

"True," Marcus conceded.

"Well, wasn't that water helping people in L.A.?"

"Yeees. But that wasn't the issue. There are lots of other systems that can be used to meet the city's water needs—much more balanced approaches. Take conservation, for example. During the drought of 1991, citizens of L.A. managed to cut water usage by over 32 percent. That's more than enough of a savings to protect Mono. When the drought became less severe, a lot of people went back to their old water-wasting habits. *That's* what bothers me. I just think it's all so unnecessary. It's not that I believe humans shouldn't consume natural resources. We *should.* That's the way it was meant to be. It's just that I believe we should use our resources wisely. Respect the one who gave them to us. Be good stewards."

More religious talk. *But I like his attitude.*

For once, the topic of spiritual matters didn't set Celia's teeth on edge. She leaned up against the Cruiser's padded seat and felt the road's vibration against her cheek. Several miles later, the gentle rocking had nearly lulled her to sleep when the sound of

Marcus's voice, filled with shock and dread, broke into her consciousness.

"No. Oh, no. It can't be."

"Marc—" Celia jerked upright. "What is it? What?"

"Up ahead. Over there." Marcus pointed, his face grim.

In the distance, black-shadowed hilltops rose against a midnight-colored sky, the point at which the first ended and the next began almost imperceptible to her sleepy eyes. Celia traced the outline of the horizon with her eyes, searching for signs of anything unusual.

She peered intently through the windshield. "I don't—" Her voice dropped then as she registered Marcus's concern. There to the right, lying low in the hills, rose the faint but unmistakable glow of fiery orange light. She swallowed. "Is it bad?"

Marcus seemed at a loss for words. "Bad doesn't even begin to describe it. Those hills are like tinder. The Sierra's been in a drought for almost ten years. It's like one giant pile of kindling."

Celia rummaged through the vast recesses of her voluminous shoulder bag, pulling out a camera and new roll of film.

"Let's get closer," she ordered. "I want to get some shots—"

"I don't know, Celia. . ."

"What?" She stared at him. "You've got to be kidding."

Marcus remained silent.

"You're not kidding? What kind of a reporter are you?"

"The *cautious* kind. You don't know what it's like up here."

"Spare me." Celia's tone was sharp. "I'll be careful. I'm not an idiot. Besides, this is the opportunity of a lifetime. The media's never *on-site* to report on a wildfire. We'll be famous!"

"I'd rather we were safe," he grumbled.

"If I wasn't here, you'd be up there in a second, isn't that right?"

Marcus stared at the road, glowering. What she said was true, she was sure. If he were alone, he'd be right up at the fire lines.

"It's because I'm a woman." She was ready for a fight now.

"It's not because you're a woman!" Marcus dragged tension-filled fingers through his hair, making it stand wildly on end. "It's because you're...*you.*"

"What? What on earth is that supposed to mean?"

"Forget it!" Marcus slammed his palms against the wheel. "Have it your way." Dark silhouettes rushed past more quickly than before.

Celia flinched at the anger in his tone but offered nothing further, unwilling to risk this opportunity to catch a firsthand glimpse of the crown of fire.

Marcus drove wordlessly but swiftly, navigating his way down the open highway then around a series of winding, dirt Forest Service roads he clearly knew better than Celia did her own neighborhood back in Atlanta.

Minutes later, the silence wore heavily on her nerves. "I guess you're mad at me, huh?"

Marcus's eyes never left the road.

"Okay. Never mind." *So much for our truce. Oh, well. It was fun while it lasted....*

The air became increasingly thick, black, and heavy as they drew closer to the fire. Along the highway, an abandoned fleet of muddy, battered 4 x 4's marked their approach to the staging area. Marcus pulled over beside a large silver Ford and threw the Cruiser into 'Park.'

"Wait here," he ordered.

"Wait here," Celia parroted sarcastically but not before his door had safely shut behind him. "What am I, a dog? No offense, Hank." She glanced into the back seat where the hound snored contentedly.

All around, smoldering snags leaned precariously toward the abandoned truck family. About three hundred yards further, Celia imagined she could see tiny flames licking at a pile of broken timber.

"Be right back," she muttered unnecessarily to Hank. Her fingers touched the door handle and she pulled back slowly, cringing at the sound of its tiny, but unmistakable, opening click. She glanced nervously out the window; Marcus was nowhere to be seen. She swung the door open and lowered one foot to the ash-covered ground.

"What do you think you're doing?" Celia jumped. Marcus's voice had teeth to it; obviously, he could barely contain his fury.

"Getting out of the car?" She plastered an innocent smile on her face.

"No kidding." The teeth were still biting.

"Right. I was…uh, coming to see what you were doing."

"Uh-huh." Marcus appeared unmoved.

"I—oh, stop being such a pill! You know I want to get some shots. Just let me go over there for a *few* minutes. I'll shoot a roll…okay, maybe a couple, and then we'll—"

Suddenly, Celia became aware of how close Marcus was standing. Her gaze drifted from the deep blue of his eyes to his muscular arms, imagining how it might feel to be pulled into his powerful embrace. Without thinking, she leaned forward slightly, her face and hands tingling with the awareness of him.

Marcus stared down at her wide eyes and trembling arms. "Stick with me," was all he said, but his voice was low and gravelly. "I couldn't bear it if something happened to you."

Celia swallowed her disappointment and nodded wordlessly.

Gently, almost timidly, Marcus took her by the hand and led her toward the campsite where several soot-blackened, sweat-drenched strike team members were filling their water bottles and loading up on C-rations. He stood before one tall, bearded, filthy man, whom Celia judged to be the smelliest of all.

"Celia, this is my buddy, Ray. He's the guy in charge of the Hot Shots."

Celia nodded, meeting his grimy paw with her own.

All business, Ray skipped the preliminaries. "I told Marcus you could look up there—" He pointed toward a still-smoking stretch of wasteland. "The fire's already swept through. But be careful, 'cuz sparks can kick back up. And watch out for shifting winds—they're your greatest enemy."

"How'd the fire start?" Celia watched as an army of workers manned themselves with shovels and saws; soldiers, preparing for battle.

"She's a lightning fire. Started at about four o'clock up there at the top of—," Ray's voice broke off as the radio at his feet crackled with life. "Gotta go. That's my lead polaski—" He turned away abruptly.

"The polaski's the guy responsible for guiding and pacing the Hot Shots," Marcus whispered into Celia's ear. The feel of his breath tickled her neck.

"Oh." She stepped away and moved back toward the Land

Cruiser. "Come on. Let me grab my camera." But as they approached the vehicle, Celia felt an odd sense of apprehension. "And I want to check on Hank." Her pace quickened.

"Hank?" She peered into an empty back seat. "Hank!" Her voice rose in alarm. A quick search of the vehicle revealed that Hank was gone.

"I don't understand." Marcus was flabbergasted. "How could he—"

"It's my fault! I wasn't careful! I opened the door and just stood there with it hanging open while you and I—while we. . ."

Marcus placed broad hands on either side of her face and traced the outline of her cheek with one rough thumb. "Relax. We'll find him. It's only been a few minutes."

"But you don't know what he's like!" Celia scanned the darkened woods with frightened eyes. "He thinks he's Columbus or something! He's long gone by now." She pulled away from Marcus's touch and moved to follow several Hot Shots who were heading toward the blaze.

"Hank!"

"Hey! Where do you think you're going?"

"What do you *think?*"

"*Unh*-uh." Marcus's voice was firm. "Ray said you could look over there. We'll shout our lungs out for him. But you are not—I repeat *not*—going into the heart of the fire."

"But—"

"*No.* Don't make me physically restrain you. You know I can do it."

Celia was shocked at his betrayal. "Fine!" Her voice dripped venom. "Just keep away from me then." She stormed off in the direction Ray had indicated. "Hank? Hank!"

Marcus followed, echoing her cry. "Hank!"

Their voices floated on the wind, indistinguishable amidst the shouts of crew members and the roar of an approaching chopper. Celia stared into the fiery distance, feeling her hope die a little with each lick of flame.

Seventeen

❧

"Still falls the rain—
Dark as the world of man, black as our loss—"
Edith Sitwell, 'Still Falls the Rain'

Marcus felt an inner heat surge in his veins as he faced the enemy before him. Fleet and taunting, individual flames leapt before his eyes, daring him to end their fiery dance.

He verified the number of crew members digging the control line. *One, two, three…six, seven, eight.* All safe. He scanned the surrounding shadows. "Hank!" The other fighters ignored his repeated cry; perhaps they did not hear. After nearly eight hours of shouting, his voice had deteriorated to little more than a croak. Marcus paused, dropped his axe to the ground, and leaned wearily against it, finally acknowledging the truth he'd been running from. The dog was lost. It was time to turn back.

Celia.

The image of her sweet face haunted him. How could he tell her that her beloved companion was gone? He replayed the feeling of holding her in his arms, imagined again the fear in her eyes transforming into outright agony.

"No!" With a shout, Marcus hoisted his weapon high in the

air and stormed deeper into the battle, determined to vanquish the enemy that had broken Celia's heart.

At exactly that moment, the rain began to fall.

Shuddering despite the heater's forceful blast, Celia trained dull eyes on the landscape ahead. The Cruiser's wipers slapped away the downpour, echoing her lament: *Hank's gone. Hank's gone. Hank's gone.* Over nine hours had passed since the droopy-eyed hound had disappeared; Marcus had been gone nearly as long. Celia turned off the engine, her five minutes of rationed warmth spent.

At first, she begged repeatedly for an opportunity to search the wooded slopes herself. But Marcus had remained unmoved, insisting, "You're not trained. You'd be lost in ten minutes. I'll go. I've worked with the guys before. I know the terrain. Besides, someone has to stay here and watch for him." Celia had felt patronized, but Ray agreed with Marcus, and knowing she was pitifully outnumbered and outranked, she had finally given in.

How can Hank possibly survive out there? He couldn't fight his way out of a paper bag. The animal's consistent response, whenever Celia would playfully drop her mohair throw over his shoulders, was simply to heave a heavy sigh, curl up on the floor, and drift off to sleep—unwilling to exert the effort necessary to work his way free.

Celia raised a hand to her lips and tried to stop their trembling. *Poor little guy.* Hank was the ultimate couch potato—except when he got the urge to roam. Yet even his most inspired wanderings could hardly be called strenuous. When the going got tough, Hank took naps. So where was he? Celia watched as yet another Hot Shot crew member staggered into camp.

And where was Marcus? A wave of nausea swept over her as she struggled to suppress the fear growing in her heart. Surely the rain was helping to bring the fire under control? Why hadn't he come back?

Stupid! Her thoughts had been only of herself. She knew Hank's independent streak well; back at Mono Lake Marcus had even suggested keeping him on the leash. Celia knew that Hank fell asleep easily; she also knew he could be awakened just as easily, which is what he must have done when she and Marcus had raised their voices. She should have been more aware.

Celia wrapped cold arms across her chest and around her shoulders. If only Marcus were here to hold her close, to give her comfort. *Marcus. Sweet Marcus.* She'd insisted on getting closer to the flames. Now *he* was the one in danger. What was she thinking? Obviously, she wasn't. How else could she have let him go?

God, please protect him.

How can I face her? Defeat bore heavily on Marcus's shoulders, its weight seeming almost unbearable. Two weeks earlier, his biggest concern was maintaining his magazine's readership. Suddenly, unexplainably, all he could think of was protecting the beautiful stranger who had waltzed onto his mountain and taken captive his heart.

She'll hate me. Marcus had wanted to make things right for Celia. All night he'd fantasized about strolling into camp, the peacefully sleeping hound lying safe within his arms. *Hail the conquering hero.* If wishing alone could have brought Hank home, the sheer intensity of his longing would have ended the search hours ago. Surely Celia realized by now that the animal was gone; yet, he dreaded giving her the final verdict.

Please, God. Help her to bear it.

Celia paced back and forth in the mud surrounding the Land Cruiser, oblivious to the rain pouring down her face in rivulets. Her suede jacket, its ruin complete, hung slack about her shoulders.

This can't be right. Concern had turned into panic. Ray had assured her all the crew members were safe, but Celia remained unconvinced. *Would he really tell me if there was something wrong?*

I don't care what they say. If Marcus isn't back in five more minutes, I'm going out there. She tapped at her watch, the numbers barely visible within its fog-clouded face. Five-eighteen. The hands hadn't moved in at least an hour.

All right. That does it. Celia stepped resolutely toward the edge of camp, fully prepared to fight her way past any Hot Shot who dared stand in her way.

Then she saw him.

Marcus trudged out from a stand of trees, shoulders slumped, his head hanging low. His entire body dripped with streams of sweat and rain. All around him, Hot Shots whooped enthusiastically and pounded each other's backs, exhilarated by their victory over the fire. In contrast to their victorious, soldierlike return, Marcus felt like nothing so much as a prisoner of war.

He raised his face and scanned the clearing, his anguished eyes quickly locating the woman who so completely occupied his mind. He opened his arms wide in a gesture of defeat.

Sandaled feet slopped through the mud as Celia rushed toward him. Marcus shook his head sorrowfully at her approach.

"It was no use. I tried—"

In spite of the sweat and grime that covered him, Celia threw herself into his arms and pressed her soft cheek against his, tears mingling with gritty streaks of soot. Timidly, she touched gentle

133

fingers to his chest, his temple, his hair…seeming to reassure herself that he was real.

"Oh, Marcus—"

Suddenly Marcus's lips were upon hers, effectively silencing her words. He could feel her relax against him, her arms pressed against the warmth of his shoulders, her mouth soft and sweet against his. Overcome by emotion, it was several long moments before either found the voice to speak again.

"Sweetheart, I'm so sorry. I looked everywhere. There was just too much smoke. It was so hard to see—"

He could feel Celia's heart pounding as he held her. He knew she was struggling to digest the news about Hank. He looked into the trusting face turned up to meet his. With her masks of humor and indifference stripped away, the woman in his arms seemed uncharacteristically vulnerable and fragile. And in her need, she was turning to him. For a moment, Marcus felt almost fearful, the responsibility overwhelming. *I don't know if I can do this. Can I really be what she needs?* But as he gazed into the deep green pools of her eyes, the claustrophobic feeling receded, and he knew, as surely as the sun shone in the sky, that he would be willing to die trying.

"Come on." He led her back toward the circle of vehicles. "There's nothing else we can do now. Let me take you home. We'll get you cleaned up, get some food in your stomach. Things will be easier to deal with after you're rested."

"Me? What about you?" Celia held his hand tightly. "You're the one who was out there all night with Smokey the Bear."

"Honey," Marcus's voice was gentle. "I think Smokey's job is *preventing* forest fires, not fighting them."

Celia smiled weakly and leaned against him. "You're right. Let's go home."

Marcus tucked Celia into the front seat of the Land Cruiser, covering her with a grubby wool blanket provided by one of the Hot Shots. With the fire finally under control, the crew members were feeling much more sympathetic, and called to Marcus that they would be glad to contact Celia if they found any clues to Hank's fate.

"No, Ray." Marcus kept his voice low. "I want to be the one you call. She needs to get some rest, and I'd like to…break the news carefully, if anything's found."

"Sure thing, Marc." Ray looked at him curiously. "This one's really gotten to you, huh?"

"Yeah." Marcus shook his head and sighed, too exhausted to attempt to hide his feelings. "This one's really gotten to me."

Eighteen

❦

"Like the dew on the mountain, Like the foam on the river,
Like the bubble on the fountain,
Thou art gone, and for ever!"
Sir Walter Scott, *The Lady of the Lake*, III

Marcus's eyes flickered from the winding highway to the still figure beside him. Not a word had crossed Celia's lips since they'd left the staging area. Black brows met over the bridge of his nose as his face twisted into an expression of deep concern.

"Celia?"

"Mm?" Shining emerald eyes stared blankly into space; her voice was soft, almost inaudible.

"Sweetheart, are you all right?"

Celia gazed back at him.

"Only about six more miles," Marcus offered, when she did not answer. "Think you can make it?"

Celia nodded. Marcus watched, then, as she raised one finger to the passenger window, and began to draw idly in the layer of film the defroster was unable to dissipate. *Good-bye. Good-bye. Good—* She stopped when she ran out of frost.

He frowned. Was that normal? The only loved one he'd ever

lost was his grandfather, and it wasn't a shock. Pops had suffered from leukemia for several years; he was prepared to die, confident he was going to a 'far, far better place.' Marcus and his parents had mourned, but at the same time felt relief that Pops's pain had finally ended. Celia, on the other hand, had apparently suffered an unusual number of losses in her young life, and Marcus was unsure of what to expect from her. He glanced over once more. Her eyes brimmed with tears that did not spill.

"Sweetheart—" He stretched out an arm and took her hand. To his surprise, he found her fingers stiff and cold and trembling violently beneath his touch. "Wha—?" Alarmed, he immediately downshifted and pulled over to the side of the road. Turning toward her, he opened up his arms. Gratefully, Celia fell into them and buried her face against the warmth of his chest, weeping unchecked tears of grief.

Her sobbing continued for nearly twenty minutes; to Marcus it seemed an eternity. While she cried, he did nothing but hold her, awkwardly patting her slender back as the salty moisture soaked through his shirt and stung the burn marks on his skin. Finally, her tears began to flow more slowly; her shaking to lessen. He took her gently by the shoulders and helped her to sit up on her own.

"Hey." He wiped a tear from one eye, effectively blackening her cheek. "You gonna make it?"

Celia nodded and raised a trembling hand to his face. "Thank you."

Marcus felt his pulse quicken. Her eyes were red and bleary, her cheeks puffy, her nose runny. Yet, somehow, he found her to be the most breathtaking vision he'd ever seen. Her eyes shone like jewels. Her lips, swollen and rosy...so irresistible.... *Watch*

it, Marc. Don't take advantage. This is a woman in mourning.
Marcus flashed Celia a warm smile, gave her hand a squeeze, and
released her, reaching for the ignition key.

Once they were back on the road, Celia gave him room to
drive yet remained near. Marcus wanted to pull over and draw
her into his arms once more, but refrained. Emotions were running dangerously high. To keep things on an intensely physical
level for long, he knew, would be playing with fire. He settled for
holding her clammy fingers within the comfort of his own.

"Do you…want to talk about it?" he offered, after several
minutes of silence.

"No." Celia's voice was sorrowful. "There's nothing to say."

"It might help."

"It might not."

"Yeah, but it might."

Celia shifted her body so she was facing the opposite window.
"It might not."

Marcus bit his tongue. He expected her to slide back down
the seat, but she surprised him by holding her ground. *Maybe she
can face this.* Her hand lay motionless in his. He took a deep
breath and tried once more.

"Hank's not the first one you've lost."

Celia stiffened. "What are you asking?"

"I'm not asking anything. Just…making a comment."

"You want me to talk, but I don't want to talk."

"Why not?"

Celia sighed. "What's the old cliché? Women want comfort,
men want to fix things. You *did* comfort me. You comforted me

wonderfully, and I'm thankful." Her voice took on an edge. "But you can't fix this. It's un*fixable.*"

"What's unfixable?"

"Me…my life…this jinx—"

"'*Jinx?*'"

"Rotten luck, bad karma…whatever it is. I think it's pretty clear, I'm not meant to love anyone." She cast him a sideways glance and tried to withdraw her hand. "You should think about that, I suppose."

Marcus tightened his grip on her fingers. "Celia, you don't believe in those things."

"How do you know what I believe?" Her voice began to rise in pitch.

"I don't," Marcus conceded. "But I do know that you are an intelligent, sharp-witted, well-balanced individual who knows better than to base her life around a boogeyman theory."

"I never said it was the boogeyman."

"Who then?"

"Leave me alone." Celia succeeded in wriggling her hand free.

"What is it you're thinking?" Marcus watched helplessly as she slid back across to the passenger position.

"I said stop it."

"Celia—"

"All *right!*" Celia ground out angrily. "If you must know, it's that precious God of yours. There. Are you happy?" She rubbed at her eyes. "You and Val talk about this wonderful God who loves you so much. Well, I'm just thrilled. That's very, very nice for you. However…." She turned away. "Your God seems to be playing a little game with me. It's called 'Let's see how much

139

Celia can take.' The rules are, anything goes. Anyone I care about can—and will—be taken away. The game is over when we find my breaking point. And guess what? *Game's over.* I quit!"

"But—," Marcus struggled. "But how can you say that? He cares about you. *I* care about you."

She turned on him. "Are you prepared to promise me you'll never leave me? That you'll always be there?"

"Wh—," Marcus stammered awkwardly. "I know I have strong feelings for you. But...we've only known each other a couple weeks. I can't guarantee—"

"Oh, Marcus." Celia sounded more tired than offended. "I'm not trying to drag a marriage proposal out of you! I'm just trying to point out—there *are no guarantees.* When you were out there, in the fire, I was so afraid something was going to happen to you! I thought, 'What if he never comes back? What if I never see him again?' And those things *happen.* They happen all the time. Hank's gone. My parents are gone. Paul's gone—"

"Paul?"

Celia ignored his implied question. "I can't let you into my life...I can't let *anyone* in. This just isn't worth it."

Marcus pulled into her driveway and parked haphazardly, his heart filling with dread. "What, exactly, are you saying?"

"I'm saying—" She took a deep breath. "Thank you for everything you did for me last night...this morning. What you did was...wonderful." Celia wrung her hands in her lap. "I've got two more inns to shoot this week. After that, I'll be taking off. Maybe hitting L.A." Marcus stared at her. "Oh, don't worry," she joked halfheartedly. "I'll use one of those water-saver shower heads." Marcus did not crack a smile, neither did he yell. His face remained blank, completely unreadable.

Celia wiped her eyes with one sleeve. "I guess there's nothing else to say. I'm sorry. About everything." Before Marcus could sort out how to respond, the door slammed behind her and she was running for the house.

"Celia!" His voice bounced off the glass. If she heard him, she did not respond. "Celia, come back!"

Celia leaned her back against the door and slid to the floor, sobbing heavily. "Why? Why, God?" she cried. "Why can't I have anyone?" Trying to compose herself, she took several deep breaths and pulled herself from the ground.

Slowly, she stepped to the front windows and pulled the curtains back a crack. Outside, the black Land Cruiser stood still, the driver nothing but a shadowy figure within. Celia held her breath as the vehicle roared to life, spun gravel, and peeled out of the driveway.

Celia turned from the window and threw herself on the sofa amidst a pile of brown and white dog hair, letting grief engulf her. *Hank. Oh, Hank!* Her companion was gone forever. And, if she judged his reaction correctly, Marcus was too.

Nineteen

❧

"Come Sleep! O Sleep, the certain knot of peace.
The baiting-place of wit, the balm of woe...."
Sir Philip Sidney, *Astropehl and Stella*, 1

No! Oh, no!" Valerie covered her mouth in horror. "Oh, poor Celia! She adores that animal. He's all she had!" The basket she'd packed for her lunch date with the photographer lay abandoned on *High Sierra's* breakroom table.

"I know. Believe me, I know." Marcus pressed against his forehead with open palms, as if attempting to physically repress any memory of Hank's disappearance. He knew he looked haggard; his eyes, pink and bleary. He had thought the struggle in the forest was endless; compared to the next two nights of torment, that night of agony seemed incredibly fleeting.

"How's she coping?" Valerie sat nervously twitching one foot.

"I don't know. She won't talk to me." Marcus's voice was somber. "And I'd hate to even hazard a guess. When I left her at the house, she was an absolute puddle. I think she might have been in shock."

"Well, then, what did you leave her for?" Valerie's tone sounded accusatory.

"Staying just didn't seem like a good idea," Marcus hedged.

" 'Didn't seem like a good idea'? What kind of excuse is that? She needed you!"

"Look, Val—," Marcus stopped and glared pointedly at her foot until she caught the hint and stopped the twitching. "I know you mean well. But you weren't there. And I'm not about to explain myself. I barely even know you! Besides, I hardly see how this is any of your business—"

"Well, excuse me, Mr. Rude," Valerie said in an offended tone. "But I rather *do* think it's my business, since according to your own account, you left my friend at her house two days ago, bawling her eyes out, and no one's heard from her since. If this were a murder investigation, you'd be the prime suspect!"

Marcus lay his head in his hands and slumped in his chair, too exhausted to argue.

Leaning back, Valerie studied him carefully. "Hey." A gentle hand touched his sleeve. "I'm sorry. That was uncalled for."

Marcus shook his head. "No, you're right. I should have stayed. I should have—I just didn't know what to do! There she was in the car, looking up at me with those huge eyes. I wanted to pull over and hold her in my arms, kiss that sweet face. But we were so emotionally charged. I was afraid I'd go too far, take advantage of the situation." He stood abruptly and began to pace. "But it wasn't just the temptation of crossing a moral line. Even something simple, like a kiss—I didn't want her to rush into my arms just because she needed a pair of arms. If she ever comes to me, I want it to be because she wants to be with *me*. It all felt so confusing. Things were so complex…I was trying to think things through.… And then she threw me over! She said 'thanks for everything' and told me to leave her alone. I wanted to go after her, but how could I? I'm not about to force my affections on a woman who tells me to get lost. She doesn't want me...wouldn't let me anywhere close."

"Have you tried at all since that night?"

Marcus glowered at her. "She as much as told me to take a hike, thank you very much." He planted himself back in his seat and deliberately kicked his feet up on the table. "So this is me...hiking."

Valerie folded her arms and considered him thoughtfully. "Sounds pretty cold."

"Cold? *Cold?*" Marcus jerked upright and planted both feet on the floor with a thud. "What do you want from me? Listen, I busted my *tail* out there, fighting all night against a *forest fire*. I could have gotten killed, you know—"

"I know," Valerie agreed.

Marcus ignored her. "—trying to save an animal, just because the woman I love—"

"Love?" Valerie's eyes lit up. "Did I just hear you say 'love'?"

Marcus sat up straight and swallowed hard. His tone suddenly became subdued. "I...I believe I did hear the word 'love' in there somewhere," he admitted. "But don't have a fit about it. I wasn't thinking about what I was saying. I didn't mean—"

"Marcus Stratton, you big coward!" Valerie accused with a grin. "What on earth is so horrible about admitting that you love her? What...like it's not obvious? Like it's not written all over your face in neon? You only battled a *forest fire* for her. What's next? Slaying dragons? Spinning straw into gold?"

"Ha, ha. You've got quite a wit," Marcus remarked dryly. "I can see why you and Douglas hit it off so well."

"Mm." Valerie's eyes narrowed. "Nice try, but—*BZZZT.*" She raised her arms and mimicked the sound of a foul call. "Subject change—incomplete."

Marcus sighed heavily. "All right, all right. So what if—I'm saying *if,* now—I do love her? It doesn't make any difference. She's so far from being able to love me—or anyone—back, it's ridiculous. She's got no family, no *'Paul'*—whatever that means." Despite his best intentions, a trace of bitterness crept into his voice. "And now she's got no Hank. She thinks she's a walking curse and is bound and determined to cut herself off before anyone else gets hurt."

"That's so *sad.*"

"Yeah." Marcus's face was a mask of frustration. "But that's not all. She's convinced that God's following her around like a little black cloud making rotten things happen to her."

"I know."

"Val, I'm worried about her." Marcus spoke urgently. "I mean, I'm *really* worried about her. It's one thing for her to push me away. I hate it, but I can deal with it. But this…this is worse. That kind of pain has to go deep. I just—"

"Give me the address. I'm on my way."

Celia wriggled and kicked against the hot, sticky linen that had twisted and knotted its length around her bare legs. Tiny rays of sunshine peeked through slatted shutters, threatening to warm the room even more than its present muggy seventy-five degrees. At midmorning in late July, it was too hot for even the most cold-blooded to remain under the covers. Yet Celia could not seem to find within herself the strength—or desire—to rise.

What possible reason was there for her to get up and face the day? Photos of the last two inns weren't due for another week. No one was expecting her. No one needed her. No one wanted her...especially since she'd scared Marcus off. But that was good. That was what she'd wanted, wasn't it? No more connections. No more good-byes. No more pain...

The sound of a distant banging aggravated her ears. *Klunk, klunk, klunk.* Celia wriggled further under the sheets. *Klunk, klunk, klunk.* The noise seemed unusually steady for a sanitation worker. Mail carrier? *Go away.*

After several minutes, the pounding ended. *Thank you.* Reaching across the bed, Celia grabbed a floppy goose-feather pillow and pulled it over her head, attempting to blot out the cheerfully invading sun.

Within five minutes, the knocking resumed, only this time it was louder, and generating from the vicinity of her bedroom window. Whoever it was, he was certainly stubborn.

Marcus?

Throwing herself out of bed, Celia grabbed the shade cord and yanked it roughly. "Stratton?"

Friendly hazel eyes smiled at her. "Sorry. Just me." Valerie's voice was muffled, the movement of her lips exaggerated, as if she were talking to a small child or someone hard of hearing.

"Oh." Celia caught her breath and opened the window a crack. "Well...good. I—didn't want to see him anyway."

"Unh-*huh*. Whatever." Valerie raised hands and nose to the sill, striking a 'Kilroy' pose. Eyebrows raised as she surveyed the disorder in Celia's room. "May I come in?"

"Oh, Val...I don't know. A lot's happened this week—"

146

"I know. I went by your office today. You stood me up." The slender blonde reached down and lifted the heavy wicker basked that held her lunch.

Celia bit her lip. "I'm sorry, Val. I clean forgot—"

"Of course you did. Who wouldn't?" Everything in the woman's tone and bearing communicated great depth of compassion. "Celia, I'm really sorry about Hank. I know how you loved him. Is there anything I can do?"

"No. I just—" Suddenly, Celia was struck by the absurdity of holding such a conversation through the window. "Sorry. Go around front. I'll meet you at the door."

Celia padded across the kitchen tile, her battered cotton slippers making a familiar slapping sound. The absence of Hank's clicking toenails echoed loudly in her ears.

She stood at the door, rubbing sleep from her eyes as Valerie approached.

"Looks like you just got up," Valerie offered.

Celia looked down at her thermal knit pajamas, utilitarian yet delicate, with a trim of Venice lace. "Uh-huh." She led the way into her tiny living room and sank into an overstuffed chair.

"You look…bad." Valerie chose the frisé.

"Thanks."

"That's okay. If you didn't, I'd be even more worried than I already am. Have you been wallowing in bed this whole time?" she questioned.

Celia stared out the window.

"You know, you can't bury yourself in there forever. You don't have to go back to work right away or anything. But it would be good for you to get out and see your friends. To talk about what happened."

Celia gave no indication that she had even heard Valerie's words.

"You know I'd have come. All you had to do was call."

"I know."

Silence hung heavily between them.

"Marcus said you didn't want to talk about it."

Celia concentrated on her feet, then, after a long pause, "What else did Marcus say?"

"He said...quite a few things actually. A few of them really quite interesting."

Celia raised her eyes. "Like what?"

"Like...things that really should come straight from the horse's mouth. I think you need to talk to him."

"I can't."

"He wants to help."

"I know. That's why I can't."

Valerie opened her mouth to speak, then stopped, as if thinking better of it. After a moment, she cleared her throat and tried again. "You're afraid, aren't you?"

Celia fought valiantly to control the tears rising from her heart to her eyes. "What makes you think I'm afraid?"

"Hey." Valerie's voice was kind. "I've been there, too. I recognize the signs." She rose from her spot on the sofa, and settled herself at Celia's feet, taking her friend's hand in her own. "You're not alone, you know. There are a lot of us out there who've been hurt...in more ways that one." Celia's slender fingers lay cold and lifeless under Val's.

"Some people we love leave," Valerie admitted. "They might not mean to. Like your folks. But it happens." She patted Celia's hand gently. "And then sometimes it seems like other people just don't care enough to stay."

"Like Paul."

"Exactly. Like Paul."

"I don't know what's worse," Celia's voice trembled. "Losing someone who loves you, or knowing you love someone who doesn't love you back." An empty feeling swept over her, and the tears began to flow in spite of her efforts to control them.

"Honey, that's what you're doing now." Valerie stared intently into Celia's eyes, as if attempting to peer into her soul. "You think you're protecting yourself and anyone else who might care about you, isn't that right?"

Celia nodded and stared at her hands.

"It doesn't matter how far you run, Celia." Valerie's tone was persuasive. "You can't stop people from caring. All that happens when you shut down is that you hurt them. Just like Paul hurt you. That's how you're hurting Marcus now."

Celia raised her head, her eyes wide.

"That's right. The man's in agony."

The tiny brunette looked incredulous.

Valerie nodded. "He's going out of his mind. I'm afraid he might explode at any moment. And he's not the only one who cares. I'm here for you, too. I want to be your friend, but I can't *make* you let me in. When you shut me out, you hurt me, too."

"I'm sorry—"

"No—" She raised a hand to Celia's cheek and wiped a tear

away. "I'm not trying to make you feel worse. Although if I thought guilt was the key to success here, I might be tempted to use it." Her laughter was light, unobtrusive. "I just want you to understand that it's not as simple as you might want to believe. Other people *are* involved. And then, there's God."

"Don't tell me you're still convinced, after all that's happened, that God actually cares about me? He even took my *dog*, Val."

"Oh, Celia! I know you're angry with him because you've lost a lot of people who you loved." Her tone then became less pleading, more direct. "But, honey, nothing is forever. Not for you, and not for anyone. Nothing is ours to keep. We can't hold people...moments...feelings clutched within our grasp. We wouldn't want to if we could—they'd spoil. We've got to enjoy them...live them...*feel* them with all our souls while they're here, then treasure the memory in our hearts once they're gone." Valerie squeezed Celia's shoulders firmly. "Don't you regret a *moment* you shared with your mom or your dad, or Hank...or Paul. There was something important about every one. Cherish your memories, but let the people go. Don't cling to what might have been. Bless them for what they were. And don't curse God because they're gone. *Thank* him that they were here."

"Like 'It's better to have loved and lost, than never to have loved at all'?"

Valerie's voice was patient. "You know, clichés become clichés for a reason. People repeat them because they're true." She pulled herself to her feet, leaned forward, and planted a sisterly kiss on top of Celia's disheveled head. Then she moved resolutely toward the door. At the top of the landing she turned, and as she did, a glimmer of light caught the tears in her eyes, causing them to shine with simple brilliance.

"Hank was a great dog," she managed. "And he had a great mom."

And with those words, she was gone.

Twenty

❦

"My heart is like an anvil unto sorrow,
Which beats upon it like Cyclops' hammers...."
Christopher Marlowe, *Edward II*

Celia wandered through the towering black giants, searching for something she could not define. A dream? A promise? The image drifted close, then, as quickly, slipped from her mind's grasp, elusive as vapor.

Beneath her feet, the ground lay dry and bare, stripped of any sign of life. Without its flourishing underbrush, the hill appeared unusually severe and rocky, the friendly Sierra, suddenly harsh and cold.

Further down the ridge, but within shouting distance, Ray's team continued in their "mop-up"—plunging unprotected hands beneath smoldering logs and piles of charcoal, searching for danger areas that could ignite into new fires in the days ahead. Occasionally, a worker's efforts were rewarded by the unearthing of a malignant hot spot. Following such a discovery, the crewman would diligently dig up and smother the embers, cooling the site with handfuls of water or dirt. But such findings were relatively few and far between. The work was backbreaking and, in Celia's eyes, incredibly monotonous. However, the men and women fully understood the importance of the routine and gave the task their complete effort and undiverted attention.

The burn site was officially off-limits, but Ray had allowed Celia to come, maintaining that her presence was hardly any less appropriate than it was on the night of the fire. Sympathetic crew members offered their condolences and provided almost complete access. They warned her about potential dangers, such as leaning snags, but for the most part, they gave her the freedom to continue her exploration, undisturbed.

Celia breathed deeply. The air still held the overbearing odor of dead forest and ash. Normally, the smell of soot gave her a sense of comfort, triggering memories of scorched hot dogs and childhood camp songs; now it filled her with intimidation. She felt the urge to hide—to run to a place where the fire could no longer touch her. But even greater was her desire for answers that might be found along the fire's blackened path.

Ahead, a hundred-foot pine stood apart from the others, separated by a small, rock-strewn clearing. Brittle spikes like blackened fish bones poked in all directions. Alone and forlorn against the backdrop of desolation, the tree seemed to Celia the perfect symbol of loss.

Reaching into her shoulder bag, Celia slipped a hand around her camera and took a step forward.

"*How* much?" Marcus clutched the phone receiver in a vice-like grip. "Excuse me. I believe we must have a bad connection. I'm not asking about Boardwalk, here…or Park Place. I'm interested in the space you've got listed in— What? Yeah, that's the one." The editor grimaced. "I see. Thanks for your time."

"Everything okay?" Two small dark eyes appeared in the

doorway, blinking nervously beneath a sticky-looking tower of hair.

"I can't believe this." Marcus spun his chair around to face his secretary. "We can't make it without a stable readership. But the readers want dazzle. They want more fluff. So I try to get us a higher profile—an office in Mammoth Lakes. Tourist paradise! Rubbing elbows with the wealthy. Hobnobbing with the elite. Dazzle? Fluff? Ha! We'd have dazzle and fluff coming out our ears."

Roused by the noise, Rob poked his nose into Marcus's office. Eva shot Rob a grateful glance and made a hasty retreat. Marcus hardly noticed and now trained his eyes on his art director.

"I can't afford an office in Mammoth!" He flung his arms expressively in the air. "And I can't afford to stay here, like the little podunk operation we've been. We haven't got the money to make any of these stupid changes! I tell you—" He buried his head in his hands. "This is just too much. I feel as if the whole world's crashing in around me."

"Hey there, friend." Rob strode over and lay a firm hand on Marcus's shoulder. "Don't you think you're overreacting just a bit? You've just started to look for a new lease. You don't know what will come up tomorrow. Besides, I'm not convinced Mammoth is such a good move for us."

"Don't start, Rob. We've been over this a thousand times before."

"I know, I know. But this is the place you love. This is home. For *all* of us."

"Rob, 'home' won't mean much to us if we're all back in the city job-hunting in a year. Or less."

"It'll work out." Rob spoke with conviction. "You'll see. It always has before. You'll think of something."

"Thanks for the vote of confidence. I could use it." Marcus's tone was bitter. "I was holding up pretty well for awhile. But the last couple weeks…Man! They've been the hardest I've gone through in a long time. It's not that *circumstances* are so much worse—although they're certainly not getting any better. But I just feel so…so *broken*. I—"

"It's *her*." It was a statement, not a question.

Marcus nodded, despair etched into each line of his face. "I can't explain it. I was going along just fine…dealing with the magazine 'upgrade'—or 'downgrade', depending on your point of view." A hint of sarcasm crept into his voice. "I wasn't in the mood to get all hung up on some crazy little fighter. But then, there she was. Beautiful as an angel…." Marcus smiled weakly, despite himself. "Cuddly as a *porcupine*…." He sobered. "And reachable as the moon."

"You know, man *did* reach the moon," Rob offered. "But he knew better than to try doing it all in one trip."

Marcus sighed, prepared for yet another of Rob's rambling stories. "What are you talking about?"

"You know. First he had to believe he could do it. That whole paradigm shift thing." Rob rubbed his hands together, warming to the subject and taking on the tone of a recognized expert. "Then he—I'm speaking, of course, of 'man,' in general—made some initial tests. When those were successful, he went on his first trip. Not to the moon just yet, but out of the earth's atmosphere and into space. It wasn't 'til later that he took The Big Leap."

"The Big Leap?"

"The Big Leap."

"You get that out of a science book somewhere?" Marcus asked dryly.

"You know what I'm saying."

"Yeah, I know." Marcus sighed. "You made your point."

The two sat quietly for a moment, contemplating.

"It probably took years," Rob added cheerfully.

"*Thank you.* I'm sure that's true."

Rob grinned. "Sorry."

"No, don't be sorry. I know you're trying to help. And, admittedly, that little illustration of yours was remarkably on target for once."

Rob nodded proudly.

"I'm just so frustrated!" Marcus continued. "You know. I would have done anything for her. I wanted to make things better for her. But she practically told me to get lost. And maybe she was right. I mean, just look at me! How can I possibly help her? I can't even make things better for myself."

"Maybe you're not supposed to." Rob shrugged.

Marcus glowered at him. "What are you suggesting? That I give up?"

"Well, now...." Rob crossed lanky arms behind his head and leaned back thoughtfully. "I don't think there's anything wrong with *trying* to do things that are right. Go ahead. Give it your best shot. You always do. Just don't expect too much from yourself. After all, you're only human."

Marcus sighed heavily, spinning his chair back to the yawning window. "Tell me something I don't know."

She sat cross-legged amidst the charcoal dust, sifting rocks and sand through slender fingers. Grit stuck under her fingernails, but Celia made no attempt to clear the dirt away. The earth felt safe and real, and she imagined herself as part of it.

Ashes to ashes, dust to dust....

The pile of cinder began to grow beneath her hands. By now Hank's body was becoming a part of the dust from which animals were created. Or was that only man? That part of her theology seemed fuzzy. Where was Hank now?

We are gathered here to honor the memory of our friend, Paul Kellum....

Celia looked around. There were no daisies. Every entity that could give up its life had already done so. She reached a hand to her head, yanked out several chestnut-colored strands, and lay them in the pile. Against the rocks, the hairs lay in waves, catching and reflecting the gold of the overhead sun.

You matter....

Green eyes surveyed the mountainside as a soft voice echoed in her ears. *Celia, you've got to know that God loves you. If he doesn't—then who have you got?*

Who have you got?

Who have you got?

In a small voice, her trembling lips began, "God, I'm gathered here to honor the memory...."

Twenty-One

※

"Love bade me welcome; yet my soul drew back…"
George Herbert, *The Temple,* 'Love'

O kay, I've got it. '**SIERRA GHOST TOWN DISCLOSED AS SECRET ELVIS HIDEAWAY**,' " Rob suggested helpfully.

Marcus stretched tanned legs, poking out from khaki shorts, and rearranged them in a more comfortable position on the top of his desk. "Nah. Not outrageous enough."

"All right. How about, '**ALIENS LAND ON MONO SHORES: MISTAKE IT FOR HOME**'?"

"Please. Another alien story? Way overdone."

"Hm." Rob chewed on his lip and tapped out a drumbeat with his pencil. "Aha! Here it is. '**BIGFOOT DELIVERS "MAMMOTH" QUINTS DURING HOLIDAY SNOW-STORM**'. Get it? 'Mammoth'? Bigfoot? It's regional, heartwarm-ing—and, best of all, *seasonal.*"

"But not true."

"What's your point?"

The battle of wits was interrupted by the appearance of a fig-ure in the doorway. Blonde and lean, he wore a Pacific-blue and brick-red Madras shirt, fitted jeans, and suede city-hiker boots, giving off an air of casual composure.

"Try '**LOCAL MAGAZINE RISES TO NEW HEIGHTS: SMALL TOWN COMPETITION SINKS LIKE LEAD BALLOON**,' " the man offered. His tone was friendly; he might have been asking the men if they knew the local game score. "Now *that* would be true."

Marcus sat up angrily but managed to retain his composure. "Really, Powell," he spoke through clenched teeth. "I'm surprised at you. Condemning yourself like that before you've even begun. How fatalistic."

"Yeah." Rob was already on his feet, looking as if he'd like to go for the newcomer's throat.

The man dismissed the art director's rumpled T-shirt and jersey sweat-clad figure with a glance. "Touché," he remarked dryly, then turned back to the magazine's editor. "Marc." Michael Powell extended his hand graciously. "What's it been? Seven...eight years?"

"More like ten." Marcus returned the man's firm grip. "I have to admit," he said a bit stiffly, "I'm more than a little surprised to see you here."

"Really?" Powell raised his eyebrows. "I'm surprised at your surprise. How could I set up shop in the area and not come see my old college nemesis?" He pushed some papers aside, cleared a place for himself, and sat on the desk's edge. "You dogged me for four long years at USC. Everything I did, you did. Only...better. Or something like that. Wasn't that the drill?" The man kept his tone amiable. "You were always challenging me to 'do my best.' And now, we can do that for each other once again. Just like old times. It's a pleasure to be running in the same circles again."

Marcus remained standing while he watched his visitor intently. "I'd hardly say we were 'running in the same circles' back then, Powell. But I don't need to tell you that. You were there, weren't you?"

"Oh, yes. I was there. You were, too. I remember it clearly. Longest three years of my life."

Marcus's face revealed no emotion. "Well, you've certainly done well for yourself since. What is it…four television stations and ten, eleven—"

"Sixteen radio studios."

"Right. And now…a magazine."

"As you say. Now a magazine."

Marcus's voice held a bit of an edge. "Seems like an odd move."

"Odd?" Powell kept his face straight. "In what way?"

"Well, by your own admission. Sixteen radio and four television stations. Print hardly seems to be your media. Seems like you'd want to stick to what you know."

The friendliness dropped from Powell's tone. "Are you issuing some sort of half-baked challenge?"

Anger flashed across Marcus's face. "I think there's plenty of challenge here for the both of us. Have you done your market research? There are readers enough to support one magazine of this type. Not two."

"I see. In other words, it's a winner-take-all sort of situation."

"You could say that."

"Hm. Well, then. May the best man win."

Rob snorted derisively. "Not likely."

Powell shrugged. "Whatever."

At that moment, a small curly head appeared at Marcus's office door. "Marcus, I—," Celia stopped and stared, wide-eyed, at the roomful of men. Looking breezy and stylish in her flax-colored linen shirt and drawstring pants, she caused all three to do a double take. "Whoa. Major bad timing! Sorry. I'll—"

"NO! Wait—" Marcus nearly climbed over his desk in his eagerness to reach her side. Powell raised an eyebrow as his rival clamored past. Marcus took Celia's small hands in his own and began, fervently, "Celia, I—"

"Marc!" Powell's voice dripped exaggerated interest. "You didn't tell me! Here we are catching up on business when, all the time, there's clearly been more important news to report. You never said a word about your girlfriend!"

Celia took an awkward step back. "I'm not—"

Marcus watched her, gauging how to respond. "No. That's right. She's just…the photographer."

"Celia Randall," she offered.

Powell continued to emanate charm. He stepped over to Celia and took her hand. "Nonsense! Obviously, this woman is not 'just' anything. Celia, if your work is even half as beautiful as you are, then you are an artist of incredible talent, indeed."

Celia stared at him. *Is this guy for real? You might want to, uh, take it back to a nine, there, fella.*

Suddenly, Marcus reached over and grabbed Celia's hand roughly from Powell's grip.

"Hey!" she protested.

Marcus glared at his unwelcome guest. "All right, Powell. I think it's about time for you to go."

Celia looked from one to the other. "Look, guys," she began, wrinkling her brow. "I don't know what the problem is, but—"

"Celia, don't worry about it." Marcus kept his eyes trained on Powell.

"Hey, Marcus. Sorry." The man backed up a step, palms raised in the air. "I didn't realize you were so touchy about your woman."

"I am not his woman!" Celia stamped her foot. "Hey! Are you listening to me?" The two men ignored her, each keeping his eyes focused on his adversary. Celia's fury began to rise. "All right. I guess I might as well lay down here on the ground, and when you guys are through, the winner can just grab a clump of my hair and drag me back to his cave."

Powell was the first to break the stalemate. "I think you were right, Marc. It's about time for me to go. I just stopped by on my way to Tahoe. And—" His lips twitched in amusement. "I'd say my work here is about done."

He turned his full attention on Celia. "Please, allow me to apologize for the scene. *And* for making you feel like Wilma Flintstone." Gray eyes danced mischievously, and Celia felt her fury begin to fade in the face of his apology.

"Thank you for that." She smiled graciously. "You're forgiven, Mister.…"

"Powell. But please, call me Michael."

Her eyes opened wide as she acknowledged the introduction. "Michael. It was a pleasure to meet you."

"All right, all right—" Marcus seemed able to control his frustration no longer. "Go on. Get out of here, Powell."

The man turned at the door with one last, gracious smile for

Celia. All that he lacked was a graceful black mount and hat to tip.

"Good afternoon, neighbors. Be seeing you." He nodded and made his exit.

Rob breathed a loud sigh of relief. "Charming guy, Marc. Really."

"Oh, he didn't seem all that bad," Celia remarked.

Seeing the storm in his boss's eyes, Rob made a hasty retreat for the door. "Be cool, man," he muttered to his friend under his breath. Then he disappeared.

Marcus stepped toward Celia, awkwardly, trying to begin again. "Celia—"

"Don't 'Celia' me." After days of missing him, Celia felt stung by his treatment of her in front of Powell. "What, exactly, was that little scene back there?"

"Don't worry about it. I want to know how you—"

"Don't *worry* about it?"

"That's what I said. It doesn't matter. I don't want to talk about it."

"But—"

"It's none of your business." In his frustration, Marcus spoke a little too loudly.

"None of my *business!* All right, fine then. Let's stick to business. Here." She slapped a plastic canister of film down on the desk, then reached into her pocket for more. "And here...and here. I have one more inn to go this week, and then I'll be out of your hair."

"Celia, that's not what I—"

"Not what you what? Look, I don't really care what you

meant." She glared at him, shooting words like weapons. *She's just the photographer.* "So you might as well save your breath."

"If that's what you want." Marcus turned away, his voice dull.

"That's what I want." Celia stormed toward the door. "I'll bring the rest of the film in on Friday."

"Fine. You can leave it with Eva. Or Rob."

Celia paused. "Where are you going?"

"Mammoth Lakes."

"Oh." She would not offer to accompany him. "What for?"

"Looking for new office space."

"What? What's wrong with the space you've got?"

"We're going high-tech." Marcus sighed. "A nice, fancy, P.R. dream, with all the bells and whistles. Right in the heart of Sierra's play land."

"I don't get it." Celia raised her hands in a gesture of confusion. "What good will a move do?"

"Nothing, in and of itself," Marcus agreed. "But as part of the whole package—the whole 'facelift,'—it will give us a new image, the potential for attention from a new market—"

"I get it, I get it." Celia sounded disgusted.

"Yeah, well…save me the guilt trip. I've got enough on my mind."

"Fine."

"Fine."

Celia stepped into the hallway.

"Wait!" Marcus crossed the room in three long paces.

"Celia, please. I know you think I'm a real toad. But give me a chance here. Just let me say twenty words without jumping down my throat."

"All right." Celia raised her eyes from her shoes and met his gaze. "Twenty." She wore a poker face.

Marcus swallowed. He gazed into her eyes and spoke with measured care. "I'd sacrifice…everything I have, and more…if I could, for one single moment, offer you a measure of peace."

Celia's face softened. Emerald eyes glistened and her small hand reached out to lightly touch his.

"You've already done that. No sacrifice needed."

"What do you mean?"

She, strangely enough, felt relaxed, open. "Just that…I'm starting to deal with things. Like you and Valerie said. I don't have the answers yet. But I do have…maybe, just the tiniest measure of peace."

Marcus opened up with a smile so warm and enveloping, Celia felt as if it might swallow her whole. He moved to pull her into his arms, but she drew back, hesitating.

"Marcus, no. I can't." She knew he could read the emotional struggle that must show clearly upon her face. "Please."

Marcus swallowed his disappointment. He placed one finger under her chin and raised her eyes to meet his.

"A measure of peace is a small miracle, Celia." He smiled. "And you wondered if God ever answered prayer."

Twenty-Two

❧

"Yet do I fear thy nature;
It is too full o' the milk of human kindness...."
William Shakespeare, *Macbeth*

H ow many will there be for dinner this evening?"
Celia smiled uneasily, recognizing the waitress as the one
who had served her during her disastrous lunch with Val.
"One, please."

The woman inclined her head graciously and led Celia to a
secluded table situated in one of the restaurant's darker corners.
Great. She probably expects me to have some kind of fit again. Celia
forced herself to dismiss the embarrassing thought and nodded
her thanks.

Less than five minutes later, roused by the loud banging
sound of the front door, she raised her head from the menu. To
her surprise, Marcus's adversary stood at the front counter, waiting to be seated. Casually he canvassed the room, and when he
caught sight of her he broke into a wide smile and strode toward
her table.

"Celia Randall," he said warmly. "What a pleasant surprise!
Do you mind if I join you?"

She eyed him warily. "Are you following me, Powell?"

He laughed. "No, I'm not. Sorry. Not that you aren't worth following. In fact, if I'd thought of it first, I probably *would* have. Unfortunately, that's not the case. I'm just grabbing a bite to eat before I head up to Tahoe."

Celia looked skeptical.

"I'm serious!" he insisted. "Think about it. I'm just passing through town. I've got to eat. The chances of us running into one another are pretty great, you have to admit. There are only three restaurants in town, and the other two had signs saying, 'SHOES, SHIRT: NO SERVICE.' "

The room filled with Celia's laughter. "All right, all right. I'm convinced. Please, have a seat."

Powell beamed.

"It sounds like things are going really well," Rob offered.

"Yeah, I guess they are," Marcus agreed, kicking his feet up on the dashboard.

"Well, then. What are you crabbing about?"

"I'm not *crabbing*. I just wish she'd let me in a little more. She's so protective."

"Big deal. So she's selective about who she talks with. There's nothing wrong with a woman protecting her heart from every yahoo who comes along."

"I," Marcus began, haughtily, "am not a yahoo."

"A yahoo," Rob countered, "is *exactly* what you are. But that's beside the point."

"Maybe it is to you," Marcus grumbled. "But you're not the one being called a yahoo here."

Rob rolled his eyes. "The *point* is that she has every right to be careful. And you have no business pushing her."

"All right, all right. I get the advice, 'Dear Rob', When, exactly, did you get to be so wise?"

"I was born wise."

"Yeah." Marcus snorted. "And I was born a monkey's—hey! That's Celia's Mustang—" He pointed. "Over at Kelly's. Let's see if she wants to join us."

"Join us? Brainstorming ideas for the next issue. Oh, yeah. That sounds like a lot of fun. Whoo-*ee!* Is she ever going to be excited!"

"Oh, hush up, you old hick," Marcus ordered. "I'll just run on in and ask."

Rob turned the wheel. "You're the boss."

Celia raised her menu and pretended to be making a selection while peeking over its edge to study the man sitting across from her.

With his fine, chiseled features and thick, sun-bleached hair, Michael Powell looked more like a Hollywood personality than a communications mogul. The man clearly had taste; even in casual attire he typified the image of impeccable masculine style. Yet for all his strong features, it was ultimately his eyes—sharp and devastating—that made him the deserved object of wide-spread female attention. Celia had always prided herself on her attraction to men of substance and depth rather than those whose greatest appeal was good looks. Yet even she found herself irresistibly drawn to the attractive man who shared her table.

Suddenly, those devastating eyes turned themselves upon her.

Catching her gaze, Powell smiled.

"Do you see what you want?" he said with too much intensity for a casual question. Celia looked slightly shocked. *Is he insinuating what I think he is? Or am I being paranoid?*

"I…I think I'm still undecided," she hedged.

"I see." Powell nodded knowingly, clearly understanding. "You're a wise woman. Never choose too quickly. You never know what you might miss if you make a decision too soon. Like Marcus, for example."

Celia nearly choked on her water. "I beg your pardon?"

Her companion appeared delighted at her reaction. "Stratton was very successful back at the university," he began. "He could have gone anywhere, done anything. There must have been twenty companies that offered him jobs before he'd even graduated. And look what he did. Started his own little rag sheet, and now it's going down. He should have considered his options a little more carefully." He shrugged. "That's all I'm saying."

Celia bristled. "You don't know it's going down! And even if it does, that's your fault, not his."

Powell looked surprised. "Oh, you think so, do you? And why pray tell is that?"

"Well, because Marcus—," she stopped, mid-sentence.

"Ah. Marcus." Powell nodded again. "Well, I suppose that makes sense. I know how men think. Their egos are huge, and no man wants to show his weaknesses in front of a beautiful woman like yourself."

Celia glared at him. "Just what are you saying?"

"Not a thing." Powell scanned the dining room as if trying to locate their waitress.

Celia looked at the man more closely. "Are you implying that the magazine's problems have nothing at all to do with you? That you're just some innocent bystander?"

Powell shrugged. "Obviously, I'm not just a bystander. I'm a competitor. In Marcus's eyes, I'm definitely the enemy and, in that regard, I'm guilty as charged. But as far as being the reason *High Sierra* is heading for disaster...I'm afraid I'm not willing to take the rap, even for an old college friend."

"It doesn't sound like you two are friends," Celia said doubtfully.

"All right," Powell conceded. "I'll grant you that. Marcus and I have always been...arch-rivals, I guess you could say."

"I see. That sounds *very* friendly."

"Oh, I'll admit, we had our moments." Powell grinned. "Marcus and I came from two different backgrounds. He was at school on a scholarship, always felt he had something to prove. I was one year ahead of him, and for some reason he set me as his target early on. Anything I had, he had to have. Anything I did, he had to do better."

Celia frowned. That didn't sound like Marcus. But then, how well did she actually know him? "That must have been very unpleasant."

"That's right." Powell sounded gratified by her validation of his feelings. "It was."

"And now you're getting your revenge. Is that it?" she accused. "Sort of turning the tables on him, taking what he's got?"

"No, of—"

"If that's the case, then just for the record, you should know that I am *not* his girlfriend."

Powell looked wounded. "I think I need to make two things very clear here. Number one, I'm a successful businessman who has been leading his own life for many years." His voice was firm. "I have better things to do with my time than settling an old score with some college pipsqueak who ran in my shadow."

Celia blinked, surprised at how incredibly convincing he sounded.

"And number two," he went on more softly, "nothing in the world could induce me to express interest in a woman I did not personally admire and feel drawn to." He looked at her pointedly. "Nor is there any power that could force me *not* to care for a woman I cared for. I am a man with a very strong heart. And that is something that *you*, my dear Celia, should know."

Celia sat in stunned silence. After Paul's hesitation, it almost seemed unbelievable that he and Powell were of the same species. She hurriedly changed the subject.

"All right. Let's say, for the sake of argument, that you're not doing this specifically to spite Marcus. Then why, of all the magazines in the world, did you pick one just like his?"

"Ah, but that's the point!" Powell pounced. "It's nothing like his. That's why he hasn't got a leg to stand on. My magazine is commercially viable. His is not. There's nothing I can do to change what Marcus has done with his publication. It's had ten years to speak for itself."

"That's right, and it's been a critical success."

"A critical success," Powell allowed. "But not a success in the marketplace. Celia—" His voice communicated unlimited patience. "Old Marc has had this pie-in-the-sky mentality as long as I've known him. He'd love to save the world. Unfortunately, what he doesn't realize is that the world doesn't want to be saved. You can only publish so much doom-and-gloom before people get sick of it. People want to be entertained. They want to be happy. They want an escape from their everyday world. No one wants to hear about problems. We all have enough problems of our own." He leaned forward. "Don't we?"

Celia sighed. "Some of us more than others."

"Ah-h." Powell stared at her with penetrating eyes. "Just as I suspected. I thought I noticed a little sadness in that beautiful face of yours. Let me guess. You've broken some poor idiot's heart, and you're overcome with grief."

Celia stared out the window. "Not quite."

"All right, all right. Give me one more shot. I'd say. . ." Powell gazed up at the ceiling thoughtfully. "You're here in the mountains escaping from the throngs of men back home who trailed you wherever you went."

"Boy, you're really bad at this." Celia kept her voice even.

"Okay. One more, one more. You…are…a princess in disguise. Your horrible, no-good father, the king, is forcing you to marry against your wishes. Some cretin who has no appreciation for your finer qualities, who acts like—," he grinned, "—some kind of stone-age barbarian."

Celia averted her eyes. "You know, you're not helping."

"Oh." Powell's face fell. "I *am* sorry. I don't mean to make light of your suffering. I'm only trying to make you laugh, lighten your mood. You don't have to tell me a thing if you don't want to." He reached out and touched her hand. "But I'm actually a good listener when I'm given half a chance. Communications major, you know."

Celia jumped in surprise at the loud bang that came from the front of the building. The hostess stood behind the counter, staring at the door.

"Protecting herself. *Being careful!* Give me a break! Talk about yahoos! The woman's in there playing patty-cake with Powell! I'm going to rip his head off! That snake—"

"Now wait a minute. Let me get this straight. You're saying that those two were actually together?"

"At the same table!"

"Talking?"

"Like a couple of old high school pals!"

"Patty cake?"

"Well...practically!"

"Are you sure you aren't jumping to conclusions? You know, maybe there's some innocent explanation for this."

"Like. . .?" Marcus fumed.

"Like maybe she's...." Rob considered. "No, that wouldn't make sense. Okay," he tried again. "Maybe she really was mad at him and went to slap...." He shook his head. "Nope. That doesn't work either. *Huh.* I guess you're right. You've really got a problem here."

Marcus seethed. "It's not just my problem. Powell is going to pay for this. He wanted a battle. Well, he's getting the battle of a lifetime."

Rob chewed one thumb nervously. "I'm getting a very bad feeling about this."

"I'm so sorry about Hank. How far away was he when they found him?"

Celia looked confused. "Found him? What are you talking about?"

"I'm sorry." Powell waved his napkin in dismissal. "This is such a delicate subject, I never should have—"

"No," Celia insisted. "*What* do you mean, 'found him'?"

"Well, of course, whenever there's a fire of this size, a team is sent out afterward to 'mop up'."

"That's right," she agreed. "I saw them."

"Well," Powell sounded triumphant. "There you have it."

"There I have *what?*"

"The fire fighters cover every square foot, looking for hot spots. They find the bodies of all kinds of animals after a fire."

"Ohh." Celia cringed.

"Sorry. You asked." He patted her hand. "Surely they told you when they found him?"

"Noo." Celia wrinkled her brow. "I was a little fuzzy there, for a day or two. But I would definitely remember something like that."

"That's strange." Powell looked suspicious.

"I suppose." Celia sunk a spoon into the French onion soup the waitress had brought. "They probably just didn't find anything."

"That hardly seems likely. Unless...."

"Unless what?"

"Unless Hank didn't die in the fire."

Celia dropped her spoon. "Don't even kid about something like that."

"I'm not kidding!" Powell protested. "It's possible, isn't it?"

"Oh, I guess anything is possible. But what are the chances of a fat, short-legged little fuzzball making it out of a fire like that?"

"About one in three billion?" Powell suggested.

"Exactly."

Devastating brown eyes twinkled. "Are you feeling lucky today?"

Twenty-Three

❧

"Ye were as a firebrand plucked out of the burning."
Amos 4:11, *The Holy Bible*

"O uch!" Powell tripped and swore as he tried to climb over one of the larger trees felled in the process of bringing the fire under control.

"You okay?" Celia called out from behind him.

"Great, just great!" he answered cheerfully. Moments later, she heard him swearing once again.

"You know, you don't have to do this with me."

"Nonsense! I would never have suggested it if I didn't want to come. I'm at your service," Powell offered gallantly. "As long as you'll have me."

Celia laughed. "What about Tahoe?"

"Tahoe," Powell insisted, "is not going anywhere. I'm sure I can finish my business tomorrow. Or next week?" he suggested hopefully.

Celia considered the man before her. Dirt and ash covered once-impeccable clothing, but Powell seemed unconcerned. His devastating brown eyes concentrated on the landscape ahead. *He really doesn't seem so bad. He didn't have to come out here with me...* "We'll see," she allowed shyly. Powell seemed so suave, so shallow. Hardly much of a threat. "It's actually kind of nice to have the company."

Powell continued to work his way forward. "The most important thing is that we find Hank, if he's out here," he called over his shoulder.

"I hate getting my hopes up."

Powell held out one hand and helped her climb over a large protruding branch, holding her slender fingers within his grasp a little longer than necessary. His smile, bright and confident, seemed to shine upon her like the sun.

"That's too bad, Celia. Because there are some things actually worth hoping for."

She averted her eyes and pulled her hand away, gently. "Hank!"

Powell followed closely behind.

"Marcus, you can't do that!"

The editor looked at Rob grimly. "Oh, yes, I can. Just watch me."

"Come on, man! Think about what you're doing! A story about two teenagers from Yosemite who saw a UFO?"

"Of course not," Marcus answered dryly. "What do you think I am? Crazy? They didn't just see it. They went for a ride."

"Give me a break!" Rob paced angrily. "No one will believe that garbage."

Marcus's fingers crashed against his computer keyboard. "Ah, but that's where you're wrong! People will believe anything. *Especially* if it's outrageous and unsupported." He shook his head

177

in disgust. "The more ridiculous the better."

"Marc—," Rob stopped circling. "We're better than this, and you know it. This isn't why either of us got into the business."

"What do you want from me, Rob?" Marcus stormed to his feet. "Am I supposed to just lay down and die? Give up everything to that creep Powell?"

"There are some things Powell can't take away."

"What? Like pride, I suppose?"

"Yeah. Exactly like pride."

"Sorry, friend, but I'm afraid I have to disagree with you there. Just look around." Marcus waved his arms. "Outdated equipment. Leaking roof. Not to mention a warehouse filled with unsold back issues." He covered his face with one hand. "Powell wanted to beat me, and he's beaten me. I'm the loser here, so I hardly see how saving my pride is a factor."

"I guess it depends on your definition of 'loser', " Rob argued. "If you ask me, I'd say the word fits our friend Powell to a T."

Marcus snorted. "Yeah, right. Rich, powerful, successful…and, oh, *so* charming."

A strange expression crossed Rob's face. "Wait a minute. That's what all this is about, isn't it? Mr. Charm got the girl, and you can't hack it." He crossed the room and stood nose to nose with the editor. "You're thinking with your heart again, Marcus. Not your head."

"Well, at least I'm thinking!" Marcus retorted. "If it were up to you, we'd stay the same old two-bit, fly-by-night operation—"

"Rant all you want. You're not going to change my mind." His voice was strained. "This idea *stinks*. And I won't do it."

A muscle along Marcus's clenched jaw twitched. "You *what?*"

Rob met his eyes, unflinching. "I said 'I won't do it.' You can compromise your principles if you want, man. But you can't force me to sacrifice mine."

"Rob—," Marcus struggled for words.

Rob backed away. "I'm not kidding. I know we're friends and all. But this isn't about friendship—"

The editor exploded. "Now, wait a minute! You better *believe* it's about friendship!"

"It's about doing what's right. It's about making a difference, doing something you believe in…something that matters."

Marcus turned away. "You sound like some kind of Pollyanna."

"No, I don't," Rob insisted. "I sound like you…five years ago, when I first met you. Even six months ago. The Marcus I know wouldn't just give up like this."

"Oh, yeah?" Marcus scoffed. "What color is the sky in your Marcus's world?"

"Well, it's probably a little rosy," Rob conceded. "But I imagine it's also pretty beautiful."

"Beauty doesn't sell, Rob. How many times do we have to go over this?"

After a short silence, the art director answered quietly, thoughtfully. "I guess we've been through it enough, huh?"

"Yeah." Marcus sounded relieved to be dropping the subject. "So let's forget about all this. We'll just do the best we can and push forward."

"Noo," Rob faltered. "I don't think you understand. I can't do what you're asking. I'll do the fair thing and give two weeks notice. But after that, you'll have to find someone else to design this swill."

"But, Rob! You're my friend. I'm counting on you!"

"Don't pull that on me, Marcus." Rob was angry. "You know I'm your friend. And on a personal level, there isn't anything I wouldn't do for you."

"But this *is* personal!"

"No." Rob stuffed his hands in his pockets and began to move away. "It's just a magazine. My value doesn't rest upon whether it's a success. I have to stick to what I believe. If you're my friend, you'll understand that." He turned at the door. "I'm sorry, Marc. Really sorry."

"Sorry!" Celia giggled as she helped Powell pull himself from a pile of ash.

"Right. How many times is that, now? See if I offer you my hand again. I'm beginning to think you're part of a Marcus Stratton plot to eliminate me." Powell's words were joking, but his voice held a bit of an edge.

Celia took a defensive stance. "It's not like I lost my balance on purpose. And besides, nobody asked you to come out here, you know."

"I know, I know." Powell sighed. "You'll have to excuse me. I'm hot and I'm tired, and I think I've had about enough."

"It is pretty miserable," Celia agreed, wiping a damp arm over her glistening brow.

"What do you say we head back to the car? It's been three hours."

"I don't know…why don't you go on, yourself? I'll just look around for another hour or so."

"Celia—"

"Michael!"

"Now, hear me out—"

"No! I mean, look!" Celia pointed excitedly to a stand of trees about a quarter of a mile away.

"I don't see anything."

"I did! I saw something move!"

Powell shook his head, assessing the terrain ahead. "Celia, I don't think—"

But she was already off and running. "Hank! *Hank!*"

"Yes, I understand, Kevin. You'd like to know things are a little more stable before moving out here. Of course. That makes a lot of sense. But if I could get you to just— What?" Marcus absently clenched one fist. "I see. Well, if you change your mind, I'd appreciate it if you'd—" The editor fell silent, listening. "All right. Well, thanks again. I hope to hear from you soon." He settled the receiver back in its cradle.

"Strike Three."

Feeling suddenly drained of all energy, Marcus lay his head down on the great oak desk. Beneath his cheek the wood felt strong; its smell comforting. He absently traced the pattern of the grain with one hand.

God, please help me.

"Oh. It's you!" Celia stopped short, disappointed.

"That's right." Ray looked up from his examination and eyed

her curiously. "I'm surprised to see you out here again, Celia. Still trying to make your peace with the fire?"

"Not…exactly," she admitted. "I'm actually looking to see if there's any sign of Hank." She gestured toward the man who had followed her as she ran here. "Michael and I thought there might be a chance he's still alive."

Powell looked slightly embarrassed. "It was just a thought—" he began.

Ray ignored the man. "Celia, I understand how you feel. But, you have to realize, the chances of that are so slim—"

"But you admit there is a chance!" Celia clutched at a straw of hope.

"Well, I suppose. But not much. As far as I can guess, the only way he could have made it is if he was—" The fire fighter looked to the horizon and pointed. "See that? Right along that ridge there's a spot where the flames went straight up into the sky, rather than sweeping through the pines. If your dog waited it out in a place like that, he might have been okay. But Celia—" He spoke gently. "We haven't seen any sign of him."

Celia refused to be discouraged by Ray's assessment. "Good! That means you haven't found his body?"

"Well, no. We haven't found the body," Ray admitted. "But there's no reason to believe that we necessarily would. Just like I told Marcus. It doesn't prove a thing."

"That's right!" Celia's voice was bright. "It doesn't prove a thing." She paused. "Wait a minute. Did you say 'Marcus'?"

"That's right."

"What does Marcus have to do with anything?"

Ray seemed perfectly willing to volunteer all that he knew.

182

"He said he'd keep you posted about what was going on. Made me promise to tell him, and not you, if we found anything." The man smiled knowingly. "He was awful worried about you that night."

"Thank you." Celia kept her voice even while Powell beamed. Oblivious, Ray returned to his work.

"Come on, Michael." Celia couldn't help noticing the amused expression on her companion's face before she marched back toward the car. "I've got to head back to the office for something. Something very important." She paused. "I don't suppose you happen to know—," Celia muttered, "—which crimes might be hanging offenses in this state?"

"Eva!" Marcus barked angrily. "Eva, where are you?" The outer office sat empty. "What is this, some kind of mutiny?" he grumbled.

He walked over to her desk and began opening drawers, poking through twice-used manila folders marked by barely intelligible writing. "ADVERTISING, ANSEL ADAMS WILDERNESS, ARTICLES I LIKED…come on, art directors…art directors… Oh, for crying out loud! What kind of a filing system is this anyway?" He slammed the compartment shut as the front door opened.

"Marcus."

He raised his eyes and cringed. "Hello, Celia. It's good of you to stop by. And how nice…you've brought your friend, Powell."

Celia's eyes widened. "Excuse me?" Powell folded his arms and moved to stand by her side.

"You look real cute there, Marcus," he baited. "You'll make someone a lovely secretary one of these days."

"Stop it!" Celia snapped. "This is none of your business, Michael."

Powell raised his hands and backed up a step. "Whatever you say."

The tiny brunette turned back to Marcus in fury. "What, exactly, did you mean by telling Ray not to call me about anything they found? Hank was *my* dog, you know. Not yours. I don't remember asking you to stick your nose in my business."

"Oh, you don't, do you?"

"No, I don't!"

"Well, I'll admit, you never said those words, exactly."

"That's right!"

"However—" Marcus rose from his position over the file cabinet and pulled himself to his full height. Throwing a look of venom at the man behind her, he took Celia by the hand and drew her down the hallway toward his office.

"Hey! Where do you think you're going?" Powell called after them and moved as if to follow.

"This is a private conversation, Powell. Keep out of it," Marcus warned.

"It's all right, Michael," Celia shouted back over her shoulder. "I can take care of this." She lowered her voice and glared at Marcus. "All right. What's this all about? I suppose you think you have to take care of everything for me, because I'm a frail little woman?"

"Well, I wouldn't have put it that way. But now that you mention it, I do remember a certain frail-looking woman who threw herself into my arms."

Celia drew a quick breath. "I don't remember *throwing* myself—"

The anger in Marcus's voice was biting. "Yes, *throwing* yourself. I remember it very well. I also remember looking down into your eyes and thinking, 'This woman has suffered enough.' I remember vowing that I would do anything I could to protect you." He took a step forward so his face was inches from hers. Celia backed up instinctively. "I remember telling Ray that I wanted to be the one to break any bad news to you. I wanted it to come from a friend. I wanted it to come from someone who cared." His eyes flashed. "However, that was *before* you spilled your guts—"

"I never spilled my guts!"

"—giving me that song and dance about not letting anyone into your life. Before you took up with that weasel out there—"

"Now, you wait just a minute! Just what are you implying? I haven't 'taken up' with anybody, thank you very much!"

The eyes that had once gazed upon her so tenderly suddenly narrowed, and Marcus's voice became like cold steel. "I don't care what you call it. Just keep it out of my office. I don't want to see it. For that matter, I don't want to see you."

Celia reeled backward as if he had slapped her.

"Celia!" The sound of a hysterical cry penetrated the stifling silence between them. *"He's here! He's here!"*

Celia ran down the hallway as the front door flew open wide and Valerie James rushed into the office bearing in her arms a blackened, but wriggling, Hank.

Twenty-Four

❦

"Whatever a man prays for, he prays for a miracle."
Ivan Turgenev, 'Prayer'

Short, stumpy legs kicked at Valerie's bare arms as Hank tried to work his way free from his protector's grasp. Celia stood, momentarily stunned, with one hand over her mouth and the other gripping Powell's broad shoulder for support.

"Hank?" The word came out in a squeak.

"Well, I'll be—" Every trace of anger drained from Marcus's face, and his eyes filled with wonder. "Thank God!"

Powell simply stared, as if unable to believe the signals his eyes were sending to his brain.

"*Hank!*" The spell broken, Celia rushed to Valerie's side and scooped the struggling animal into her arms. "Oh, *Furball!* Are you okay?" She looked at Valerie anxiously as Hank weakly licked her face. "Is he all right?"

The veterinarian shook her head in amazement. "It's a real-life miracle! He's suffered smoke inhalation and he's horribly dehydrated." She pointed to a spot of bare skin on the dog's back. "Look here—he's even singed. But as far as I can tell, he's basically fine."

"Where did you find him?" Celia examined every inch of the emaciated animal.

"The Wileys brought him in to my office. Hank just kind of wandered into their yard this morning, five miles out of town, out toward Tioga Pass."

Celia's face glowed. "I can't believe it! He's okay! He's home! I never even thought there was a chance—" She dragged her eyes away from her beloved pet and cast them upon Powell. "You were right! Some things *are* worth hoping for!"

Powell looked momentarily taken aback. He looked over her shoulder then and threw Marcus a self-satisfied smile. He slipped one arm around Celia's waist and drew her close as Stratton's face grew pale. "Of course I believed." His lips were close to her ear. "Hank had something incredible to live for. Who would ever willingly leave you?"

She stared at the man who had unwittingly spoken such key words. *"Thank you."* Her voice became even warmer. A loud clatter sounded behind her as Eva's chair crashed to the floor. Celia turned.

Marcus was gone.

Celia lay stretched across the bed on her stomach, peering down at the small, furry body under her nose. Hank groaned as she scratched his upturned belly, wriggling his right front paw uncontrollably as she hit one 'sweet spot' after another. She smiled at the sound of one particularly contented wheeze.

"What are you trying to say, O Sultan?" she queried. "Would you like me to peel you a grape?" The moment was broken then by the sound of steady knocking. "Excuse me, your Royal Highness," she apologized. "That must be your pizza. Either that, or the Exalted Court Physician, James. I shall return."

Celia was not prepared for the figure who stood on the porch.

"Are you alone?" a subdued Marcus asked.

"*Yes*, I'm alone." Irritated by the implication of his question, Celia nevertheless gave in to exhaustion and resisted the urge to argue.

"May I come in?"

"I thought you didn't want to see me anymore."

"Please." His voice was urgent, all traces of anger gone.

"Well...all right. For a moment. Just don't disturb the Sultan."

Marcus smiled weakly, understanding her inference. "And get my head cut off? I wouldn't dream of it."

They settled themselves in the living room, sitting awkwardly opposite one another.

"Tea?" Celia offered, mostly to break the silence.

"No," Marcus waved her off. "Nothing, thanks. You've got enough on your mind without having to worry about entertaining me. I just came by to say—" His voice dropped off and uncomfortable silence filled the room.

"Is this the part where you apologize?" Celia prodded.

Marcus nodded. "I'm sure it is. I'm just not real certain where to begin." He raked his fingers along his scalp. "How exactly did things get so bad between us?"

Celia did not move or speak.

"It started with Powell, didn't it?"

"Marcus, if you're going to start making ridiculous accusations again—"

"No!" Marcus stopped himself, then lowered his voice and tried again. "No. I'm not. I'm just saying…you came to see me in my office this morning, and before we even got to talk, Powell and I started going at one another. I never gave you a chance to say what you wanted to say."

"That's all right," Celia assured him. "Actually, I didn't have anything particular in mind. I'd gone up to the burn site this morning and was feeling a little better about things." She smiled timidly. "I even had a little service for—well, Hank, my folks…and Paul. I even talked to that God of yours."

"I thought maybe you had." Marcus nodded. "From what you said about peace. Peace has to come from somewhere."

"You think so?" Celia considered. "I never really thought about it like that, but I suppose you're right." She glanced toward the bedroom door. "I'm still in shock."

"Because Hank's home?"

"Mm," she assented. "And because God heard me this time."

Marcus leaned against the back of the sofa. "What's so different about this time?"

Celia raised a thumb and forefinger to her temple. "I don't know…I can't imagine. You know, I'd prayed before, that God would heal my mother. That he would make things work out with Paul. When my father died, and then my mom, the pain was just beyond anything I could deal with. I felt like I couldn't take it, and I begged God to help me. To make the pain stop. But he didn't. And when I asked for help with Paul, he just ignored me."

Marcus looked concerned. "What did you expect God to do?"

"I don't know, to make Paul see things differently. To make

me see things differently. To make it stop hurting so much! I'm not really sure. All I know is that I felt like he let me down. But now look what He's done!" Celia's face was bright. "He brought Hank home, safe and sound! I've been a skeptic for a long time. But even *I* have to admit—that was a miracle."

"It certainly was," Marcus agreed. "So I guess you're convinced there's a God, after all?"

"I guess I am." Celia sounded amazed.

Marcus studied one thumbnail. "Well, I just hope he remembers."

"Who are you talking about?"

"God."

"Wh—what, exactly, do you hope he remembers?"

"Well, to perform miracles, of course." His tone was subtly, but clearly, sarcastic.

"Okay," she gave in reluctantly. "I'll bite. Why?"

"Well, because if he doesn't do miracles, then he's not God, of course." His tone was offhand, casual.

"I never said that," Celia responded quietly.

"Oh, you didn't? Huh. That's not the way it sounded to me." Celia stood abruptly and moved to stand by the window. Marcus followed her with his eyes. "Celia, listen to what you're saying. You want to trust and believe because he did something the way you wanted him to. But when things felt out of control, you blamed him for everything that went wrong."

"If he's really God, he can change things if and when he wants to," she said quietly.

"Listen to yourself! 'If he's really God….' Celia, if he's really God, then it doesn't matter what he wants to do, or why. He's

God. What do you think that means? God means *omnipotent.* He knows what's best, what's right. If he allows something, then he has his reasons. 'I know the plans I have for you, saith the Lord. Plans to prosper you, and not to harm you.' If God's really God, then he's *always* God. That doesn't ever change, even when we don't understand what's he's doing." Marcus moved to join her, and together they looked out at the bright evening sky. He pointed beyond the Milky Way. "God's out there, Celia. But you can't set any limitations or standards on him. Don't make God prove himself. He's already granted us far more than we deserve." His voice held a trace of sadness. "How can we complain when we don't always get what we need—" He lowered his head, and deep blue eyes held hers. "—when he's already given us the greatest gift of all?" Demanding no response, he turned away. "And now—where was I, before I rudely interrupted myself? Ah, yes. An apology."

Celia watched as he strode confidently across the room and stepped out the front door. When he returned, he held in his arms a brilliant bouquet of fresh wildflowers wrapped in newspaper. Her eyes opened wide.

"There aren't any florists in town—," he began.

He brought me flowers....

Celia beamed.

You matter.

Marcus winked jovially into her smiling eyes. "There, now, Celia! What more could you possibly want than this? A wonderful career, a devoted dog, a fresh bouquet, and the complete repentance of a total fool." He leaned forward and whispered, as if sharing a great secret. "Uh...that would be me."

She grinned. "So I guessed."

"I'm not sure whether to offer a sweeping apology, or to confess my sins one by one."

Celia pretended to glance at the clock. "I don't know if I've got that kind of time…but you can give it a shot."

"You're very kind." Marcus stepped forward and knelt at her feet. Celia watched, amused, as he cleared his throat and took her hand. "A-hem. Celia Randall," he began, "for my many heinous crimes, I offer my most sincere apology. For passing judgment on your relationship with Powell—," Marcus winced, but kept his tone light. "And for implying that there was anything taking place of an inappropriate nature, I am sorry. For snapping at you at the fire, and in my office, and—well…wherever else I snapped at you, I humbly apologize. For saying that I did not want to see you again—" He tightened his grip on her hand. "I ought to be shot. Uh, is there anything I'm forgetting here?"

"Undoubtedly."

"Oh. Well, consider that sweeping, all-purpose apology in effect from this point on. Agreed?"

"Agreed."

"Forgiven?"

Green eyes danced. "Forgiven."

"Uh…a hand up please?"

Celia laughed and pulled on his arm. "You're getting awfully good at this apology thing."

"Yeah…well, I've been getting a lot of practice," Marcus said ruefully. "Mind if I check in on the patient?"

"Not at all." Celia led him down the hallway to where Hank peacefully snored.

"If that isn't the most incredible sight in the world," Marcus spoke in a loud whisper, "then I don't know what is."

Without thinking, Celia took one step forward and leaned against his side. Instinctively, Marcus slipped one arm around her shoulders and looked down at her protectively, surprise revealed in his face.

"I—didn't get a chance to do this earlier today," she said, hugging him tightly.

"I didn't know you wanted to."

"Of course I did," Celia assured him. "Are you kidding? After everything you did for me the other night? I feel as though somehow, you were responsible. That you were in the right place, at the right time, and something you did made it possible for him to survive."

"I see." Marcus rubbed her shoulders gently. "So what you're saying is that you see me as some sort of a guardian angel for your dog?"

"Mm…more or less." Celia grinned.

Marcus stared deeply into her eyes. "I can think of someone I'd be even happier to protect—"

The moment was interrupted by a sudden knocking at the door. Hank awoke with a loud *whoof* and tried to rouse himself from the bed.

"Oh, Hank! Don't!" Celia pulled herself from Marcus's embrace and moved to the animal's side. "Stay put." She turned back to Marcus. "That's the pizza. Valerie told me to take it easy on his stomach, but I thought a couple of bites couldn't hurt him. You're welcome to join us if you can keep our secret."

Marcus bowed at the waist. "The Sultan's wish is my command."

Celia grinned. "I think the Sultan wishes for you to get the door." She watched his retreating back and whispered in her dog's ear, "I know, I know. He's a little strange. But I think I kinda like him."

Twenty-Five

❧

*"Like one, that on a lonesome road
Doth walk in fear and dread...."*
Samuel Coleridge Taylor, *The Ancient Mariner*

H ey, Rob. How's the cover piece coming?" Marcus poked his head into his friend's office."

"Right on track." Rob spun around on his stool to face him. "Celia's taken some great shots. You know, she's really good."

"Wonderful!" Marcus grinned from ear-to-ear, feeling strangely pleased and proud. "What've you got so far?"

"Over there, on the drafting board." Rob pointed.

Marcus walked over and studied the layout carefully. "Very clean," he approved. "Nice lighting. Interesting angles. And the mood is...." His voice trailed off.

"Hard to describe, isn't it?"

Marcus nodded. "It's different. Not sad, exactly. Almost...lonely, but in an appealing sort of way...like it's calling out to the reader. How does she do that? It's mostly just a bunch of empty rooms."

Rob shrugged. "What can I say? It's art. She's good."

"I guess *so*." Marcus turned away from the table and moved as if to leave.

"But that's not all." Rob stopped him with his words.

Marcus paused at the door. "What do you mean?"

His friend pulled a stack of black and white prints from his desk drawer. "When Celia gave you those rolls of film, did she mention anything about developing some personal photos for her?"

"No...." Marcus considered. "I don't think so. We didn't actually talk about the film at all, if I remember right. She was mad about something." He laughed. "I'm lucky she didn't just throw it at me."

Rob raised his eyebrows. "Yeah, well, it looks like we've got an extra bonus. One of her rolls was shot up at the burn."

"Oh, yeah?" Marcus gave Rob his full attention now. "Anything interesting?"

"Don't know. Guess it depends on what you mean by 'interesting.' There's nothing worth selling to the papers. No evidence of arson or careless campers. But when you look at it with an artist's eye, like I do...."

"All right, all right already, Mr. Art Critic. *Out* with it."

Rob held out the pictures in his grip. "Take a look at these."

Marcus took the prints from him and scanned through the pile of stark images—a desolate, charred pine, once-grassy fields now barren, and acre after burnt acre of charred forest. The images were simple; yet as he studied them, Marcus felt the sudden chill of loneliness.

"These are incredible."

"Yeah, they are," Rob agreed.

"And they're so...."

"Sad?" Rob supplied.

Marcus remained silent.

"Just like the woman, wouldn't you say, Marcus?" Rob prodded. "Beautiful. But sad."

Beautiful. But sad. Marcus had to agree. The words were a fitting description. He flipped through the stack once again, this time examining each print with greater deliberation. Finally he announced, "I think Randy should see these."

"Who...Olmstead?" Rob looked surprised. "The guy with the big studio up north?"

"Yeah. He's putting on a show for some of his protégés this fall. I have a feeling he might be interested in Celia's work."

Rob let out a low whistle. "You're crazy, man. That guy must have dozens...no, *hundreds* of artists trying to get his eye. You can't get him to look at Celia's stuff at this late date."

Marcus grinned enthusiastically, delighted at his idea. "He's a friend, Rob. Friends help friends, right?"

"Well, yeah. But you've always tried not to get involved in the whole 'who knows who' artist scene. Are you sure you want to call in a favor like this for someone you hardly know?" Rob challenged.

Marcus spoke with confidence. "You know, I never understood this before. But when you care about someone enough, Rob, it doesn't feel like a sacrifice, or a favor." Rob's face mirrored the surprise and amazement evident on his own as the declaration fell from his lips: "It just feels like...*love.*"

Twenty-Six

◦◦◦

"She bid me take love easy, as the leaves grow on the tree;
But I, being young and foolish, with her
would not agree."
W.B. Yeats, 'Down by the Salley Gardens'

Truth or dare?"

"What?" Marcus looked at Celia as if she might be in danger of losing her mind. "I go to all the trouble of putting a lunch together—no small feat for me, I might add—driving all the way out to your house—"

"What, twelve blocks?"

"—picking up you and Lazarus here, and bringing you to one of the most beautiful mountain hideaways in the world. Not to mention *giving you the day off*—"

"Uh, excuse me. But I think you *did* just mention it." Celia took an enormous bite of ham and cheese.

"What's that?"

"Yoo sed," Celia managed around her mouthful, "nod to menchon...." She swallowed carefully. "That you were giving me the day off, and then you mentioned it. That's cheating." She wiped tiny white crumbs from the smug expression on her face.

"Don't change the subject."

"Me?" She waved her sandwich in the air. "Ha! I think you're the one trying to get out of this. The challenge was, truth or dare?"

"Come on, Hank," Marcus pleaded with the animal laying at his feet. "Get me out of this. You've lived with this woman for awhile now. You must know how to control her." The hound remained motionless.

"Sorry, bub." Celia sounded anything but sympathetic. "Looks like you're on your own. Unless…you're chicken?"

Marcus seemed to watch her in delighted amusement. Laying sprawled upon a beautiful Indian blanket that matched the green of her eyes, Celia felt, for the first time, perfectly relaxed and carefree.

"You know, peer pressure isn't something to be taken lightly—"

Celia waved one arm regally. "Quit stalling! Pick!" she ordered.

"All right, all right." Marcus glanced around the meadow. "I don't see a whole lot around here that could get me into trouble. I guess I'll take dare."

"Aha! You have just sealed your fate!" Celia's laugh was ominously sinister.

"Uh-oh."

Minutes later, Celia rolled across the blanket in laughter at the sight of Marcus playing wild air guitar and singing a passionate rendition of "Hound Dog" before Hank's critical, sleepy eyes.

"Ouch!" she interrupted, waving her arms, after his second

chorus. "Enough already! You are *way* off key—"

"I beg your pardon?" Marcus stopped in the middle of one sweeping windmill stroke, looking indignant.

"And besides," Celia continued. "I'm not so sure Hank should be hearing this song." She looked protectively at his lazy form. "I mean, what kind of message is that? 'You ain't never caught a rabbit, and you ain't no friend of mine?' If you ask me, that sounds like conditional love. What animal can live up to those kind of expectations?"

Marcus considered the slothful animal at his feet. "I'll bet the only thing Hank could catch is a cold."

"Hey! Watch it. He's very sensitive about his lack of hunting skill. He's much more of a—well, a thinker, if you will."

"A thinker."

"That's right. And anyway, I'd like to see *you* catch a rabbit."

"I'm sure I could be a perfectly competent hunter, if I chose to be." Marcus sniffed and moved to sit beside her.

"Yeah, right," Celia grunted. "Visions of Elmer Fudd come to mind."

"Ahh—I'd watch it if I were you," Marcus warned. "You're acting awfully cocky for a woman who hasn't even taken her turn yet."

"Huh?" Celia blinked innocently and moved to rise. "Oh, didn't I mention? I need to be getting back—"

"*Uh*-uh." Marcus pulled her back down. "Not even a good try. What's your poison? Truth…" He raised his eyebrows, grinning wickedly. "Or *dare?*"

Celia pictured herself dancing dizzily around the meadow like some kind of crazed, three-footed sugar plum fairy, or worse.

"Uh...I'll take truth."

Marcus looked surprised. "You? *You?* You'll take truth?"

"Yes, truth." Celia realized her tone was a bit cross. "You don't have to say it like that."

"Like what?"

"Like the last thing you expect in the world is for me to be honest about something."

"Sorry," Marcus grinned. "It's not that. It's just that you always seem so...unreachable," he finished.

"Mm," Celia considered. "I guess I have been pretty closed off with you, huh?"

"That would be one way of putting it."

Celia looked into the gentle blue eyes that held hers. "I suppose I haven't been real fair. Tell you what. You get one freebie. Anything you want to ask, I'll answer."

"Anything?"

"Anything."

"No matter what?"

"No matter what."

"Well—," Marcus began, then stopped himself. "You know, you don't have to. Just because we're playing this stupid game. I don't want to make you—"

"It's okay," Celia assured him. For the first time in months, in the brisk mountain air, beneath smiling sunny skies, and under Marcus's warm gaze, the idea of opening up seemed more appealing than threatening. "I want to." Timidly, she touched his sleeve.

"All right, then." Marcus covered her fingers with his own.

His eyes were compassionate, searching. "So tell me…whatever happened with this guy, Paul?"

She stared at him for a moment. "Boy, you don't start small, do you? You pull out the big guns."

"Celia, don't—"

"No. It's all right." She buried the fingers of her free hand in the coarse hair on Hank's back and thought for a moment. "You know how these things happen when you're not looking for them? I remember, when I was younger, my girlfriends and I would wish and hope and worry that we'd never find someone wonderful. It seemed so important to be in love, to be lovable. But then, I just reached a point where it didn't seem to matter so much. I mean, I still liked the idea of being in love. But it just didn't seem to be my whole goal in life. I finally decided that despite what all of my well-meaning friends and relatives said, we weren't put on this earth just to pair up and propagate the species."

"So what was your theory about why we *were* put here?"

"I wasn't really sure. Come to think of it, I'm still not. But I think it has a lot more to do with how we live our lives than anything else. I don't think a person has to be married or have kids to feel complete."

Marcus furrowed his brow. "You don't think being married is a good thing?"

"Oh, no!" She shook her head vehemently. "That's not what I meant. Marriage and kids are great. I just don't think that's where life begins, or that if you don't have them, you don't have a life of worth. I don't believe we need other people to make us whole." Celia gazed up at the blue expanse overhead. "At least I hope not," she whispered.

"It sounds like you put a lot of thought into this." Marcus's tone was light, gently probing.

"You have to when you're alone." Celia's voice was dull. "What am I supposed to believe? That God has someone for everyone who deserves it, and I didn't measure up?"

"*Is* that what you believe?"

Celia considered thoughtfully. "I think I did for a long time, after Paul. It felt like a crummy trick. After years of being alone, God showed me someone who brought real light into my life. It wasn't just that he was handsome or intelligent or charming—although Paul really was all those things. He was incredible." Celia was so absorbed in her story, she barely noticed when Marcus slipped his hand away.

"There was something about Paul I can't explain. The moment I met him, I felt like I knew him. He definitely had his bad points. He was a horrible workaholic. Incredibly single-minded. Sometimes I felt totally dispensable. Like he could go days, weeks, without seeing me, and not even care. But when we were together...." Celia's face lit up. "I felt safe and warm. Being in his arms was like...like being where I belonged. Like coming home. He had this way of looking at me, and his eyes would get all crinkly. And it was like he saw me like no one else saw me. Like a work of art. Like something precious and rare. I believed he could see beauty in me no one else could see." Celia still felt reverence for the wonder that was Paul. "Even when he was cranky. Even when he was impatient. Underneath this rough exterior, was this gentle, tender man whom I loved more than anything. When I laughed, he was the one I wanted to laugh with. When I cried, he was the one I ran to for comfort.

"Things were pretty serious between us for a couple of years.

We were the perfect match. Everyone expected us to get married. Even me." Celia shook her head ruefully. "When we first met, I was thoroughly miserable—working as an office assistant for this insulation company—and just doing photography part-time. But Paul believed in me. He always told me I had talent. Encouraged me to freelance full-time." Her green eyes caught Marcus's and held them. "I did, and that was the beginning of everything in my career. He believed in me with all his heart, Marcus." Her face fell. "And I thought that he loved me. But when it got right down to setting the date, he pulled back."

"Why?"

"Why. Why? Huh. That's the question every jilted lover asks, isn't it? And the answer is always the same."

"What?"

"I wasn't good enough."

"That's ridiculous!" Marcus exploded. "Do you actually believe that every time a couple breaks up it's because one of them wasn't good enough?"

"No."

"Well, then—"

"But in my case, I think that's really what happened."

Obviously unable to sit still, Marcus rose angrily and began to pace. "Just because you don't see any other explanation doesn't mean one doesn't exist."

"It doesn't mean it *does,* either." Celia climbed to her feet and planted her hands on her hips.

"Why are you so *stubborn?*" Marcus fumed.

"Why are you so sure it wasn't my fault?" she challenged.

Marcus seemed to be struggling for just the right words.

"Because—," he began. "He—," he tried once more. "If I—" Finally, in exasperation, he stepped across the blanket and pulled Celia close, responding with an argument more convincing than words.

After several long, tender moments, he pulled his face away from hers and spoke breathlessly but rationally, his emotional frustration eased. "Because any man who would walk away from you would have to be the biggest fool who ever lived. When you walk into a room, Celia Randall, it's as if someone has opened up a window." His deep blue eyes glistened. "The sun shines a little stronger. The day seems a little brighter. Even the most breathtaking background becomes dull. Every detail fades in comparison to the color of your hair—" Marcus curled one chestnut tendril around his index finger. "The sparkle in your eyes—"

"Marcus—" Celia began to pull away, uncertainly.

"No!" he silenced her protest with a firm, but gentle kiss, and held her fast. "I'll let you go, but not until you hear me out." His words reassured her, and she relaxed within his arms. "That's better. Now, I've listened to what you've said, Celia. And I understand. You've experienced a great deal of loss, and it's understandable that you feel like it's because of something you've done or been." Gentle fingers traced the curve of her cheek. "But whether you can see it or not, you are valuable. You're *wonderful.* You're not some incredible actress with a flawless persona. You are who you are. I can see you. Really *see* you. Inside and out." Marcus's deep smile reached his eyes. "And I like what I see." He relaxed his hold but only slightly. "I know you're hurting. But you can't shut down forever. Love *will* come to you again. That's one thing I know." The timbre of his voice sounded odd, strained. "Please don't turn your back on it when it does. You've got to start believing again."

"Believing in what?"

"Believing in yourself. In your own worth. In the worth that you have in God's eyes. The worth that I can see in you."

"Marcus, I don't know—"

"It's okay." He patted her back gently, as if comforting a small child. "I know it's hard for you to accept. But I'll help you. I'll make you see."

Celia stiffened. "You'll 'make' me see. . .?"

"That's right," Marcus spoke confidently. "You're not used to knowing that someone really loves you. But I *do,* Celia. And once you understand that—"

"Stop it, Marcus." She pulled from his arms, abruptly.

"What?" He looked genuinely confused. "What's the problem?"

"The *problem,*" Celia enunciated clearly, "is that I am not some broken vase you can just sweep up and put back together. Just because you think you understand what's wrong with me doesn't mean you necessarily know what's best."

"Yes, I do." Marcus's voice barely masked his growing exasperation as she turned away. "*I'm* what's best for you. Because I love you." He stared at the back of her still form. "Did you hear me, Celia? I said I love you. I said it *twice.*" He was clearly angry now. "Or does that mean anything to you?"

"Of course it means something to me!" She spun to face him. "How cold do you think I am? But you're asking too much! Too much! I've tried to tell you, I'm not ready. Not yet. I'm not healed—"

"I know! I want to help you—"

"It's not your place!" Celia was aware that her words were

hurtful, but she could not seem to manage to bite them back. "You're not God. You can't heal me!"

"That's funny. You know an awful lot about God all of a sudden, for someone who's turned her back on Him."

Celia sucked in her breath. "That's not fair, Marcus! I haven't—"

"Oh, you haven't?" he challenged.

Suddenly, Celia felt numb. She lowered her eyes, closing him out, almost like she was closing the shutters on the windows of her soul. Marcus had gone too far.

"It's time to go back." Celia quickly gathered up the basket and blanket and, without waiting for his response, hurried off in the direction of the car.

Twenty-Seven

❧

"En tout choses il faut considérer la fin.
In all matters one must consider the end."
Jean de la Fontaine, *Fables,* 'Le Renard et le Bouc'

Bright black eyes peered over the tall desk, like a bird tracking the advance of a slow-moving beetle. "I wouldn't go back there if I were you."

The front door shut behind Celia with a bang. "Sorry…what was that?" She blinked, trying to adjust to the dim office lighting after her afternoon in the glaring Sierra sun.

Eva blinked right back. "He's in a snit." She jerked her head in the direction of the back offices.

"About what?" Celia glanced nervously in the direction indicated.

"The question," Eva confided in a low voice, "is not what he *is* in a snit about, but whether there's anything he *isn't* in a snit about. He's running the whole gamut today. UFOs.…"

"UFOs?" Celia shook her head, wondering if she had heard right.

"…office space. Loyalty and friendship. Let's see. Oh, yes! The availability of decent—much less *good*—art directors.…"

"Art directors? Wh—? Oh, no. Don't tell me *Rob* is leaving?"

"*Mm*-hm." The blinking increased in speed. "And to hear it, you'd think he was guilty of murder." Eva bobbed her head vigorously. "Temperature's about thirty below back there, if you get my drift."

"I get your drift. But I think I'll have to brave it. I've got my last roll of film here. I'm already behind schedule because of the fire, and Marcus has been waiting—"

"Suit yourself." The woman shrugged. "But watch out for the chill." She gave Celia a look of pity and turned back to her sagging in-basket.

"Thanks." Celia mustered her courage and stepped gingerly down the hall, hoping for an opportunity to assess the situation before being noticed.

As it turned out, assessment from a distance was easily accomplished, as Marcus's voice could be clearly heard through the building's thick log walls. Celia stood quietly, ten feet from his office door, pressed up against the hallway wall like a child playing 'international spy.' She bit her lip and glanced back over her shoulder hoping that Eva would not turn around at her desk and discover her eavesdropping.

"Come on, Rob!" Marcus's voice boomed. "Don't do this to me. I can't get anybody but Jack Springer. I can't use Jack Springer!"

Celia heard the soft, unintelligible response of a somewhat calmer art director.

"You know very well why!" Marcus continued. "He's so…predictable!"

Then, after a short pause, "Yes, I want to give the people what they want. But I don't want to be predictable in how we do it! There must be a way we can reach some kind of compromise."

Celia held her breath.

"For crying out loud!" Marcus's voice grew markedly louder, and Celia instinctively took a step back, away from the open doorway, as if he were advancing upon her. "You keep coming back to that stupid UFO story. Why can't you just think of it as...I don't know, *humor?*"

Again, the mumblings.

"I can't!" Celia could picture Marcus now, characteristically running fingers through his thick hair. "You know that. Even if I wanted to. I've already made arrangements in Mammoth. We've announced the proposed changes to the trade journals. The ball is already rolling, Rob. Stopping it now would be suicide."

Celia heard Rob utter a brief response, then she started when he appeared abruptly in Marcus's doorway. She inched closer to the wall as Rob rushed past, muttering under his breath, "—more than one kind of death, isn't there?" Without a backward glance, he stormed out of the building.

Suddenly Celia became aware of a curious black-eyed gaze. She relaxed self-consciously against the wall and, under Eva's watchful stare, smoothed her skirt and waved cheerfully before advancing toward Marcus's office, trying to act like a polite guest waiting her turn, rather than the prying snoop she knew she was.

Laying one hand upon the smooth doorjamb, she took a deep breath and peered into the room. For the first time ever, she found Marcus seated properly at his desk—not with dangling legs, nor with propped up feet, but with shoes planted firmly on the floor, his back straight and stiff.

His strong, but gentle features bore obvious signs of strain, and Celia became suddenly aware of how different he looked from the day she had first arrived. He seemed older, the lines around his eyes and mouth etched more deeply than she remembered. Even in three short days he seemed to have become paler. The tan remained, yet looked flat; his natural color—particularly that in his face—seemed dull, faded.

"Excuse me?"

Marcus looked up, roused from his concentration by her voice. Then he returned his eyes to the papers on his desk. "I'm very busy, Celia. Is there something you wanted?"

She hesitated. For days she'd battled feelings of guilt and longing, and struggled to prepare herself for the pain she knew would be evident in his eyes. His dismissive attitude now caught her off guard. "I…have something for you." She stepped forward, her tiny fingers wrapped into a ball.

Marcus watched her approach, staring at her outstretched hand. Slowly, her fingers unfolded before him and she watched him focus on the small black object she held in her hand.

"Film," he commented stupidly.

"Yes." Celia reached into her purse. "And…I've three more films. I mean rolls. Of film." She stumbled over her words, looking slightly rattled. "This is the last inn, Marcus. I'm…done with the job."

Heavy lids closed over eyes that showed their first trace of suffering. Marcus remained silent for several moments, then opened his eyes again, all signs of emotion gone. "That's fine. If you'll just leave it here on the desk, I'll have Rob take care of it. You might want to see him before you go. I guess you got one of your own personal rolls of film mixed in with the rest. I'm sure you'll want them returned." His voice remained emotionless. "You can leave town in a day or two, once we've had a chance to check the proofs. There shouldn't be any problems. We've gotten something we can use from each of your earlier rolls. But you can never be too careful."

"I...hadn't really made plans to leave yet." Celia faltered, unsure herself of what she was trying to say. Marcus kept his eyes trained upon the folder in his hand. She glanced around the room nervously and clenched her fists at her side, accidentally cracking two knuckles. The noise startled her, and she spoke quickly to cover her embarrassment. "But I suppose now, I will. I mean, there's no point in sticking around." She paused, waiting for a cue from Marcus. "Is there?"

Marcus finally raised his head to meet her eyes. But his face gave nothing away. "I guess not. Unless...you can think of some reason you might want to stay?"

"Well..." Celia bit one rosy lip. "You might need someone for a few days to help you with the move. To Mammoth." She gestured awkwardly. "For the magazine."

Marcus watched her closely. "Is that the best reason you can think of for staying?"

Celia lowered her gaze and drew a line on the carpet with one scuffed sandal. She knew what he was asking. As much as she hated the idea of leaving, and as much as she wanted him to give her a reason to stay, she couldn't bring herself to say the words she knew he wanted to hear. *Not yet. Why can't he just throw me a lifeline here?*

"I don't know. It seems like a good enough reason to me."

Now Marcus lowered his eyes. "Thanks for the offer. But I really don't think I need any more of your help." His tone was cold.

"Oh." Celia felt a chill creep down her spine. She shuffled her feet uncomfortably. "Well…I'll be around for at least one more day. You know where to find me. In case…you need me." She looked embarrassed. "About the film."

"About the film. Of course." Marcus scratched something on a notepad.

"Well," Celia repeated. "Thank you. For everything. Hank—"

"I believe you've already thanked me." His voice still held no emotion.

"Right. So I guess that's it, then." She began to back away. "I…appreciate the job. It really is beautiful here. You were right when you said there was no other place like it." Her eyes darted around her as she stepped toward the door, and words rushed from her mouth in a flood. "Not that I know, really. I mean, I've been a lot of places, but I haven't been everywhere, of course. How could I have been everywhere?" She laughed nervously, the sound small and sickly in the quiet of the room. "Still, I can't imagine anyplace being quite like this. Or anyone quite…like you." Her eyes sought his, pleading, but Marcus kept his focus on a pile of contracts in his hand.

"Well. I hope everything turns out the way you want it to," she finished lamely. "Good-bye, Marcus."

Silence was her only farewell. She left without another word.

"Come on, Hank. You're *not* cooperating." Celia leaned across the bed and lay nose to nose with the sluggish animal. "I'm trying to pack, here. Can I get a little help, please?" Nudged softly by her fist, Hank rolled easily toward a pile of socks, allowing her to pull from beneath him a hair-covered, mango T-shirt. Carefully, Celia shook off the brown and white fur and folded the material, still warm from the dog's body.

"The sooner we're ready, the sooner we can bail this joint, once the boss man gives us clearance. So what's it gonna be, hmm?" She scratched his furry muzzle. "Seattle? San Francisco? L.A.?" Hank raised his eyes but lay motionless. "Come on. Here's your chance! I don't want to hear you whining later because you didn't get to vote."

Sighing heavily, the hound closed his bloodshot eyes and settled himself against the soft blankets.

"Refusing to participate, huh? Well, we're not staying here, that's for sure." Celia turned her head toward a sound at the front door. "There's Auntie Val. You stay put." Following her instructions, or ignoring her, Hank remained in one spot, wheezing contentedly.

"Hey!" Valerie smiled brightly. "I got your message. Lunch, huh? What's the occasion?"

"Uh…come on in, Val." Celia waved her friend inside. "Well, today you have your choice. We can go out to Kelly's again, and I'll try to maintain my composure." The blonde laughed. "Or we can just hang out here."

"Hm. What've you got?"

"How do you feel about tortellini salad and French bread?"

"Mm. Perfect!" Valerie looked around the room. "Where's Trouble?"

"I believe Master Hank is reclining in the boudoir."

"Ah." Valerie nodded. "I see. May I see him?"

"Of course."

After performing a brief examination of her patient, Valerie joined Celia at the kitchen table where heaping plates of pasta and wedges of thick, crusty bread awaited.

"So what's the verdict?" Celia poured two tall glasses of iced tea.

"Well, you know what they say—love is the best medicine. He's making an amazing recovery."

"Love, huh? I thought it was laughter."

Valerie waved a forkful of pasta. "Yeah, sure. For *people*. But when was the last time you saw a dog laugh?"

"Good point."

"That's right. They've got to heal somehow." Hazel eyes twinkled. "Might as well be love."

For the next twenty minutes the two women talked and laughed about a variety of subjects before the subject turned back to Hank once again.

"By the way," Valerie interrupted herself. "That reminds me. I think you should know your dog is making a real mess in there."

"Pardon?"

"He's acting like a bird or something. Making a nest out of all your clothes."

"Oh." Celia took a deep breath. "Actually, that was me. I'm...packing, actually. The job's over, Val. Looks like I'm leaving tomorrow."

"Wha—?" Valerie choked around her tortellini. "Isn't that a little...sudden?"

"Noo. Not really."

The blonde lay down her fork, her meal forgotten. "But you said you wanted to move out west!" she said helplessly.

"I do! I *am*," Celia assured her.

"Well, where are you going?"

"Maybe L.A. I haven't decided."

"Well...but—"

"Valerie. You know I can't stay here."

"I don't see why not!" The other woman looked exasperated. "You travel around all the time anyway. What difference does it make where your home base is? You've got friends here. You've got me to look after Hank—"

"I can't."

"Give me one good reason why not."

Celia leaned forward. *"Marcus Stratton,"* she enunciated clearly.

"Oh." Valerie looked thoughtful. "All right, then. Give me *two* good reasons."

Celia laughed despite herself. "Valerie—"

"No, I'm serious. You can't just run off every time some guy likes you, for goodness' sake."

"That's not it—"

"Oh, it's not?" Valerie pushed.

"No!"

"Really?"

"Really!" Celia began to look agitated. "Look, I need to be...closer to supplies. I need to be making contacts. I—"

"Yes?"

"Oh, all right! You want me to say it? I need to get away from that man!"

"Why?" Valerie reached across and squeezed Celia's hand.

"Why are you so scared of him?"

"Because…. Oh, Val! I just have been through this so many times before. You care about someone. You let them in, they become a part of you. And then they get ripped away, and there's no going back. I know it sounds unreasonable. Believe me, I *do!* But I just can't help it! I feel as if I just couldn't take it one more time. If I lost one more person I loved, I think I'd just crumble up into a little ball and die."

"I know you feel that way." Valerie's voice was sympathetic. "But honestly, Celia. You wouldn't die."

"Well maybe not. But I'd wish that I had."

"Maybe. But at least you would have *lived* in the meantime."

Celia thought for a moment. "Well what if I did? Care about Marcus, I mean. How do I know he'll even like me once he really gets to know me? How do I know something won't happen to him, and I'll be left alone again? And even if things worked out, and we got *serious*—as hard as that is to imagine—" She rolled her eyes. "How do I know he won't just up and leave me a couple of years down the line?"

"Well…you don't."

"Exactly!" Celia folded her arms and sat back, triumphantly.

"That's right. *Exactly.*" Valerie met the challenge in her eyes. "There's a risk involved. *That's* what makes it all worthwhile. Nothing good ever comes easy, Celia. If you plan to always make comfortable choices in life, then you're in for some real disappointments.

"You know, you can run if you want to. Go someplace new. Start over again." Her voice took on an edge. "Try a little harder next time not to let anyone close. You can be cute and funny, and keep people at arm's length. But there will always be friends who care, whether you want them to or not. That's human nature." She gestured enthusiastically. "*That's* what makes us different from every other animal species. It's not that we can grow and adapt to our surroundings. Big deal. So can plants. It's not just that we have a sense of right and wrong. Or that we can process complex issues. That's a great quality, but even computers can solve problems."

Valerie's voice became softer, but her tone remained firm. "Celia, you asked me once if I believed in God? Well, I *do*. I believe in Him. And I believe that we are made in His image. And that means that *we can love.* For centuries, men and women have debated the meaning of life. But you know what I think? I think we're here to love. To love God. Each other. Even *ourselves.*" She reached across the table, dragging a sleeve through the remainder of her tortellini, and grasped her friend's two small hands. "Celia, you *are* lovable." Her eyes were pleading. "Give yourself a break! Don't isolate yourself from everyone who cares about you. You've got to take risks. If you ever want to feel the joy of love again, then you'll have to open yourself up to heartache."

Celia's eyes pooled with tears. "Like, 'It's better to have loved and lost than never to have loved at all'?"

"That's right," Valerie assured her. "Remember what we said about clichés? More often than not, they're *true*. What you're feeling is totally normal. You want to draw in, close up, isolate. Put up walls. It's like you're shouting, YOU CAN'T HURT ME IF I DON'T LET YOU. AND YOU CAN'T MAKE ME LET YOU! Well, you're right, Celia. No one can make you open up. And if you *do* let people in, sooner or later, someone is bound to hurt you again. But that doesn't have to make you crumble! One person's response to you doesn't determine your whole worth.

And besides, one person's love can't sustain you, anyway. Your value isn't determined by man. It's determined by *God*." Valerie smiled and shook Celia's hands gently. "You have immeasurable value in God's eyes. No matter what you do. No one else's feelings or actions can change that." She looked at her compassionately. "But, honey, no one can make you believe it but *you.*"

She rose from the table and began to gather her things. Celia followed her uncertainly to the door. At the landing, Valerie turned and threw her arms around the younger woman.

"Oh, I am going to miss you around here, Celia Randall!"

"I'll miss you, too," Celia offered sadly. "I feel like we could have become such great friends."

Valerie looked at her in surprise, then pulled her close once more.

"You goose!" the woman chastised kindly. "As if I'd let a little thing like you moving away come between us!" She sighed. "I suggest you save your 'could haves' for Marcus."

Twenty-Eight

❧

*"O villain, villain, smiling, damned villain
…One may smile, and smile, and be a villain."*
William Shakespeare, *Hamlet*

Eva! Where's the complete list of advertisers?" Marcus roared. "*Eva!*"

The black-haired woman approached his office like a first-century Christian about to be fed to the lions.

"I set it on your desk this morning," she offered timidly from the doorway.

"I said the *complete* list." Marcus waved the paper in his hand and scowled. "There are only *eight* on this sheet."

"I know. We've only got eight sponsors committed for the next issue." She blinked, waiting as if for the explosion she knew would follow.

"*Eight?* Eight! Well, great! That should just about pay for our *closet space.*" He glared at her. "What are you thinking, Eva? Get on the phone with our regulars and see if you can convince anyone to sign an agreement."

Eva's voice rose in pitch. "What do you think I've *been* doing, Marcus? I can't make anybody sign if they don't want to sign."

"Well...use your head, why don't you? Offer them a break in rates."

Black eyes, usually gentle, now flashed. "If you're so smart, why don't *you* call? I'm sure they'd rather talk to you anyway."

"And what is that supposed to mean?"

"It means—," Eva spoke clearly, and in comparison to her usual speaking voice, rather loudly, "—that the rates aren't the only problem in getting people to sign." The blinking increased.

"Eva," Marcus began testily, "if you're trying to say something, I'd appreciate it if you just came right out and said it."

"All right, then. Here it is. Everyone knows you're changing the format, and they're not quite sure why. They don't know what it's going to be, and they're not too sure they'll like it. Most importantly, they don't know whether or not our *readers* will like it. They're holding off, to see what happens. And I don't blame them one bit."

Marcus rubbed one rough, callused hand over his face. "I know, I know. To be perfectly honest, I don't either." He sighed. "Eva. What am I going to do?"

"I don't know, Marcus," she responded quietly and turned to go.

"Wait! Eva—" Marcus met her at the door. "Look, I'm sorry for being so hard on you. This isn't your fault. *None* of it's your fault. Rob's, either."

"I know." Eva spoke simply, with dignity. "Why don't you tell that to Rob?"

Marcus nodded. "I suppose I should. Augh! This is so frustrating! And embarrassing. I've been awfully hard on him—and on you—haven't I?"

"Yes, you have," she agreed. "It's been a rough couple of months for you, I know. But you stayed pretty decent until just recently. In the last couple of weeks, you've turned into some kind of editorial monster."

A smile tugged at the corners of Marcus's mouth. "I've been called worse." *That…idiot nearly ran over me and my dog!* Green eyes and dark curls danced in his mind's eye.

Eva smirked. "You don't know the half of it!" Looking more at ease, she turned on her heel, then stopped abruptly, and stood face-to-chest with Michael Powell.

"Excuse me. May I help you?" She gave the stranger a disapproving stare.

"That's all right, Eva" her boss interceded. "I'll take care of this. Powell?" The woman raised her eyebrows at the mention of the man's name as Marcus motioned for him to follow.

Once inside his office, the editor shut the door behind them. "All right, Michael." Marcus felt himself blushing and his muscles tightening. "Let's have it. What do you want?"

Powell settled himself on the broker's chair and gave a low whistle. "Whew! No wonder you had to apologize to your secretary. You are getting ruder and ruder these days, buddy."

"I am not your buddy," Marcus informed him through clenched teeth. "And I am not being rude. I'd simply like for you to state your business so we can get this over with. I'm a busy man, Powell."

"No doubt." Powell gave Marcus a long, slow smile.

"Spit it *out*, Michael."

"All right, all right. I just wanted to find out how I could get ahold of your girlfr— Oh, excuse me!" The blonde raised one hand to his lips, as if embarrassed. "Celia's not your girlfriend, is she? Sorry. My mistake." A satisfied grin spread across his face. "I forgot."

A muscle in Marcus's jaw twitched. "And just what makes you think for one minute that I'd be willing to help you find her?"

His adversary shrugged. "It's a small town. If I drive around long enough, I'll probably find her myself."

"Maybe she's already gone."

"Maybe," Powell allowed. "But I think you're acting a little too nervous for that to be true. It doesn't matter. Either way, I'll find her. But when I do, I'll have to tell her all about how I had a job for her—a nice, juicy environmental piece—you know, a little added fluff, *color* for the magazine—" Marcus's eyes flashed. "But you wouldn't refer me." Powell smiled innocently. "Of course, then you'd look even more small and petty than you do now. But then, she's probably not likely to think any less of you than she does already."

"You don't have the faintest idea what she thinks about me."

"Oh, I don't? Hm." Powell scratched his chin. "You know, the other night at dinner, she seemed pretty sympathetic when I told her what a little leech you were in college."

"You *what?*"

"Oh, yes." Powell nodded. "I told her how jealous you were. How you had to take away everything I had, just so you'd feel like big man on campus."

"Oh, come on! That's not the way it was, and you know it!" Marcus stormed. "There was plenty of challenge—and credit— for the both of us. And for everyone else in the department. You just didn't like the fact that someone else was making a name for

himself. Success always came easy for you, Powell. Way too easy."
Marcus spat out his words in frustration and anger. "I never
meant to make things harder for you. But if I did take you down
a peg, I'm glad. Welcome to the real world. Nothing good comes
easy. *That's life.*"

"Life, hm?" Powell pinched his eyebrows together, as if in
deep thought. "Well, I'm afraid I can't say that Celia saw it that
way. As a matter of fact, when I told her about your behavior, she
was quite enlightened, and very supportive of my position. I
think she called you…now, what was the word she used? Oh,
yes. 'Unpleasant.' And from what I've seen today, I'd have to
agree with her opinion. Your secretary probably would, too. If
there's one word that describes you, Marc, I'd say it's *unpleasant.*"

"*Get out of here,* Powell." It took supreme effort for Marcus to
control his temper.

"Oh, come on, Marc—"

"I'm not kidding. If you know what's good for you, you will
remove yourself from my office. *Now.*" If Powell didn't leave on
his own, Marcus felt quite capable of physically throwing him
out.

But Michael did not appear threatened. "If you say so,
Marc." He strode, unhurried, to the office door. With his hand
on the brass knob, he turned and bestowed one last, glowing
smile. "Don't worry, old buddy. I'll give her a kiss for you." And
he wisely made a hasty exit.

Looking out the window to monitor Powell's departure,
Marcus realized, too late, the error of his timing. Below him, on
the street, Celia's car approached, just as Michael was exiting the
building. Marcus watched helplessly as Powell strutted toward
the Mustang and engaged the beautiful photographer in a brief

conversation. Then, after speaking with Powell for several minutes, Celia smiled sweetly, rolled up her window, and stepped out of the car. The editor stared, dumbfounded, as she raised one graceful arm and pointed from herself to Powell, then to the open baseball field. Marcus turned away from the window, feeling his heart turn cold.

"I'm glad I ran into you, too." Celia smiled. "I wanted to talk with you about something."

"Wonderful!" Powell beamed and drew her arm through his, matching her smaller steps with his own. "I can't imagine a more perfect day for a walk...or a more beautiful companion." He glanced up at the building across from them, and his smile grew.

Celia tugged at her arm gently, then decided it might be less trouble to leave it within Powell's grasp. "I...wanted to thank you again for your support over Hank. A friend of mine has been talking with me about how important it is to love others." She laughed. "I know she was talking about *people,* but all I can think about these days is how much I love my dog, and how close I came to losing him. I guess it's easy to overlook how much we care for someone until they're really gone." She fell silent.

"I know exactly what you mean." Powell's voice sounded heavy with emotion, but there was no real warmth in his eyes. "It wasn't until I reached Tahoe that I realized how much I wanted to be with you." Celia's steps slowed. *Oh, no.* Her companion stopped short and turned to face her. "Celia, you are a beautiful woman."

"Uh...thank you." She glanced around uncertainly.

"I hurried back as quickly as I could, to find you," he continued dramatically. "And it's a good thing I did. Marcus wasn't about to tell me how to get ahold of—"

"He wasn't?" Celia was suddenly very interested in what he was saying.

"No, he wasn't." Powell peered at her through narrowed eyelids. "I told him I had a job for you, but I'm afraid he didn't seem inclined to give you a favorable reference."

"Oh." Celia lowered her eyes. "What did he say…exactly?"

"Don't worry about it. I never pay attention to anything Marcus says." Powell took a deep breath and tried again. "Celia—"

"You know, I'm glad you brought Marcus up."

He drew back slightly and cast suspicious eyes upon her. "You are?"

"Mm-hm." Her eyes softened. "Actually, that's what I wanted to talk about with you. I'm worried about him."

Powell cocked his head, looking incredulous. "You've got to be kidding. Worried?"

"That's right. You know, you've got an awful lot of stations to put your energy into. All Marcus has is this *one* thing that he cares about—his magazine." She touched his arm gently. "Please, Michael. I know you and Marcus were rivals. But you have the power to do something wonderful here…to give him another chance. Pick some other topic for your magazine. Or just go back to your stations. But, please…leave Marcus alone."

Powell shook his head slowly. "I'm sorry, but I'm afraid I can't help you there. The decision isn't just up to me. My board of directors—"

"Yes, but surely they listen to you! Tell them you've conducted more research and found that the market isn't as profitable as you'd originally anticipated. Tell them you don't think it's economically feasible to publish a magazine out here with the resources at hand. Tell them…tell them you've changed your mind. Just tell them something! Please."

Powell pulled away. "What is this? National 'Save Marcus' Day? I told you, Celia, I can't do it. Now, can we please just drop the subject?"

"No!" Celia grasped at Powell's arm, unable to shake the image of Marcus, bowed low over his desk, nearly beaten. "You're the only one who can make a difference. Surely, you must know Marcus is a good man. The things he does matters. *He matters.*"

"He matters?" Powell stared at the increasing desperation in her voice.

"Yes, he matters!" Celia wiped away tears of frustration.

"I can certainly see that he does." Michael grimaced, his lips tight and thin across his teeth. "You're in love with old Marc, is that it?"

"Wh—?" Celia looked alarmed. "I never said—"

"No you didn't. But that's hardly necessary, is it? Look at the state you're in! How sweet." All friendliness was gone from his tone. "You're trying to save your man."

Powell's words rang in her ears. *You're in love with old Marc…you're in love with old Marc…you're in love with old Marc.*

She looked up. "It isn't any of your business. And there's no need to be sarcastic."

"Ah, but I'm not being sarcastic. I think what you're trying to do is really very wonderful. In fact.…" He looked thoughtful. "I believe there's nothing I'd like more than to be loved by someone the way you seem to care for Marcus." He reached out and stroked her cheek. "I think I'd like that even more than having my own magazine."

Celia jerked her head away. "What is that supposed to mean?"

Powell scratched his chin, faking a pensive attitude. "Oh, I don't know. I think I'm a reasonable man. I don't expect to have everything all at once. Once I have my own magazine, I imagine I won't have time for love. But if I had the right woman—" He turned and eyed her hungrily. "I don't suppose I'd even need some ridiculous magazine."

"You…are…sick!" Celia covered her mouth with one hand and backed away. "I can't believe you would even suggest such a thing!"

"Careful, Celia," Powell warned, his penetrating eyes focused. "You were wrong when you said I was the only one who could make a difference in Marcus's life. You see, *you* are the one who has the power now. It's up to you how you will use it." He moved toward her. Celia backed up, but he reached her in several long steps and caught her arm in a tense grip. "By the way, I would suggest that you not say anything negative about me to our friend Marcus. Marc has always had a big mouth. If he got any strange ideas, I'm afraid he might be tempted to spread all kinds of rumors about me in the industry." Powell raised his eyebrows. "Which would, of course, sound like sour grapes coming from the editor of a questionable magazine that has no funding. And I know my lawyers have plenty of other work to concentrate on, without adding Marcus's tiny little complaints to the list." He pulled a small card from his pocket and pressed it into Celia's hand. "Here's my number in Tahoe. I look forward to hearing from you. Soon." Smiling like a Cheshire cat, he turned and walked back toward the road.

In anguish, Celia raised her eyes to the window across the street. Not a soul was in sight.

Twenty-Nine

❦

"Intreat me not to leave thee."
Ruth 1:16, *The Holy Bible*

I can't believe it!" Celia hugged her pudgy dog to her chest. "*This,* my friend, is exactly why I don't like the idea of being in love." She turned his weighty body and nuzzled him, nose to nose. "Trouble. With a capital *T.*" When his ears perked up, she nodded. "Yeah. That's right. It figures you'd recognize that word."

Celia lay the animal back down on the bed and rolled away from him, wailing, "How can this even be *happening?*" Landing on her stomach, she dangled her body over the edge of the mattress, feeling the rush of blood to her head. "I feel like I'm the weepy damsel in some cheesy old melodrama, and the rent is due."

"Ugh!" She pulled herself back up and punched one large goose-down pillow. "What a *weasel!*" She flopped down and lay staring at the ceiling, considering what to do. *Talk to Hank, as usual?* The animal gave her an outlet for her emotions but, admittedly, offered little feedback. *Marcus?* Celia shuddered. The mention of Powell's name could only raise trouble in that court. *Valerie?* They'd already said good-bye, and Celia hated the idea of going through their farewells all over again. Besides, she could already imagine the sort of advice Val would be likely to give.

After considerable deliberation, Celia slid off the bed and knelt stiffly beside the foot board. Pushing away Hank's curious, wet nose, she cleared her throat nervously and spoke out loud, "Lord, I…uh, guess it's been awhile since I've come to you. I can't imagine that you'd want to hear from me after all these years. But…I feel awfully alone. And I've been thinking a lot about what Valerie said. About you loving me. And I really hope it's true." Her lips and voice trembled, and she clasped her fingers together tightly. "Please, *please* let it be true.…"

When she walked into *High Sierra's* office that afternoon, Celia found Eva in the midst of a packing frenzy. Boxes, broken down, stood stacked against the front wall; half-filled cartons lay at strategic points along the floor causing sizable road blocks for the agitated secretary. Celia stared at her, astonished.

"Eva! What is going *on?*"

"Marcus found us a place in Mammoth." Eva grunted, ripping off lengths of tape. "And it's available *now.* So we're going, *now.*" The woman coughed, probably a reaction to the strong smell of cardboard and the dust particles in the air.

"I see." Celia nodded toward the back. "Is he in?"

"He's in," Eva confirmed. "But he is *not* happy. Watch your step, sweetie."

Celia walked toward his office taking deep, measured breaths. *It's okay. You can do this.*

"Marcus!" She entered the room smiling brightly. "My goodness! It looks like the packing fairies have invaded!"

Marcus glanced down from his perch on top of the steplad-der, pulling books off the uppermost shelves. He swallowed hard. Celia, dressed in knee-length, cut-off denim shorts, a poppy-colored tank, and ratty white sneakers, felt suddenly self-con-scious.

"Hi, Celia." He stared at her face, but his voice was still the monotone she had come to expect. "I'm glad you're here."

"Yeah, I can tell." She laughed.

Marcus wiped his hands on his jeans, ignoring her attempt at light humor. "You got a phone call here this morning. Number's on the corner of the desk. There." He pointed. "On your right. Name was Randy Olmstead."

"Randy Olmstead. Randy— Oh!" Celia's hand flew to her mouth. "Not from Seattle?"

"That's the one."

She filed through the papers he indicated and clutched the note to her chest. "Oh, Marcus! *Marcus!* May I use your phone? Randy *Olmstead.* But he's the—"

"Yeah, yeah. I know. He's got a big studio up north. It seems that someone passed on some of your work to him, to be consid-ered for a big art exhibit he's got coming up." Marcus's mouth turned up slightly at the corners.

"Yes? And?" She hung onto his every word.

"Well, he didn't like them." A grin spread across Marcus's broad face. "He *loved* them. And he thinks that *you* have a tremendous amount of potential."

"Oh, Marcus!" She ran to the stepladder, and although he reached toward her, he almost lost his footing and wound up awkwardly shaking her hand. "Congratulations. Looks like you're on your way to becoming a huge success." The dark look fell over his face once more, and he withdrew his hand from her small one, retreating back to his seat on the top rung. "I guess Powell is rubbing off on you."

"Oh, Marcus—" Celia tugged gently at his cuff, but he pulled his leg away.

"I hope you'll be happy in Seattle." He turned his attention back to the books. "Rob says your last shots were fine, so you're free to go whenever you'd like." Celia took a step back as if she'd been struck. "I would imagine the sooner the better. Olmstead said the show's in just a few months, and I'm sure there will be a lot of work involved in getting ready."

"But *Marcus*—," she tried again.

"Oh, and by the way. . ." Marcus looked down from his ladder once again. "Speaking of Powell, he said to tell you hello."

"I've already seen him," Celia snapped. "This morning. And—"

"Oh, no." Marcus seemed determined not to let her get a word in edgewise. "Not this morning. This *afternoon*. It was after your stroll across the street."

"Our 'stroll'? You were watching?" Celia looked appalled. She remembered how Powell had taken her arm and walked beside her, a little too closely, how she'd pulled away angrily and looked around for help.

"Please." Marcus's tone was dry. "'Watching'? I have better things to do than spy on you and lover boy."

" 'Lover boy'? Oh, now, Marcus, really! This has just gone too far."

"Please, Celia." He sounded disgusted. "Don't defend him to me."

"But I wasn't *defending* him—"

"You know, your arguments might mean something if I cared about this thing between you and Powell. But I don't. All right?" The words were cutting in and of themselves; his tone gave them extra bite.

"You…don't?"

"No. I don't."

"Really?"

Marcus glowered at her. "Really." He spoke emphatically. "Powell wanted me to tell you that he was looking forward to your call." He reached for another dust-covered book, then turned back to her once again. "Oh. One other thing," he said calmly.

"Yeees?"

"You might as well know that Powell told me what you said. I know what you think of me." Marcus glared at her, his anger becoming more and more apparent. "And I know what you did."

"Oh, really? And what did I supposedly say and do?"

Marcus brushed a dusty hand against his leg and began to climb down the ladder. "Well, now, that's the interesting thing." A trace of sarcasm slipped into his voice. "You see, I'm not all that concerned about what *Powell* says about me. After all, I know what his opinion is. And frankly, I don't care."

"I understand." Celia watched carefully, trying to anticipate what might come next as he lowered himself to the floor.

"The surprising thing was what *you* said about me. After all that's happened, I realize you may think I'm a real idiot—"

"Marcus, *no*—" She started to step forward, then stepped back, knowing her touch would be unwelcome.

"But even if you don't want us to be together…" Marcus's look was cold. "I thought that you at least *liked* me. That's why it was such a shock."

"What are you talking about? What do you think I said?"

"Let me see.…" Marcus pretended to search his memory. "Oh, yes. Well, he mentioned this morning, while he was here, that at dinner the other night—"

"He invited himself to my table, Marcus. I didn't ask."

He ignored her explanation. "Anyway, the two of you were talking, and he was telling you about what a vulture I was at USC, when you volunteered that you found me very unpleasant."

" 'Unpleasant'?" Celia blinked, remembering.

"'*Unpleasant.*'"

"Well…I may have used that word. But I'm sure he's repeating it out of context."

"I'm sure. You know, Celia, I have only the nicest things to say about you. This is a small industry. If you can't do the same for me, I wish you'd just keep your mouth shut."

"But Marcus—"

"And then, of course, there was that thing about the magazine."

"Oh!" She sighed, exasperated. "Now what? What *thing?*"

"What thing?" He rolled his eyes. "I suppose you don't know what I'm talking about?"

"No, Marcus. Stop that! I *don't* know. What's the problem now?"

"You're telling me that you didn't have a special request for Powell this morning?"

"Well, yeees. I suppose I did," Celia wavered.

"What? You're not sure? What exactly did you say?"

"I…asked him to back off," she admitted.

"I'm not a charity case, Celia!" Marcus exploded. "I don't need you to go begging to your boyfriend, asking him to *back off*. I can take care of myself, *and* my magazine, thank you very much. You can keep your pity. *And* your charity."

"Marcus! It wasn't *pity*."

"Oh, really?"

"Yes, *really*."

"Well, then what was it? What on earth would induce you to humiliate me like that, begging on my behalf?"

"Because I care about you! There, I said it! Are you happy?"

Marcus ceased pacing and stood motionless, as if he had just been turned to stone. After several long, heavy moments of silence, he finally broke into the quiet. "No, of course I'm not happy," he said in a low voice. "Just look at you!" He stared at her in anguish. "Looking at me with those huge eyes of yours, looking so sad…telling me that you care. What am I supposed to do? Everything about you says, 'Don't let me go.' But you know how I feel, Celia! I've told you I love you. And now you say you care about me." He thrust his hands deep into his pockets as if to keep himself from pulling her into his arms. "But what does that mean if you don't want to stay?"

"I never said that I didn't want to stay. I just said that I couldn't *promise* to stay. Forever. Don't you know what that would mean?" Celia cried. "You may care about me now, but if you thought you had me, you wouldn't want me anymore. You'd feel trapped. Restless. And then you'd leave."

"Celia, I wouldn't—"

"And even if you didn't leave, you'd probably *wish* you could leave, but feel like you couldn't, which is actually a lot worse, I think."

"Celia," Marcus tried again. "Just because someone else left you doesn't mean that I will."

"I can't risk it. I'm not strong enough. I feel like I'm just barely beginning to heal. I don't think I could take another heartache."

"I don't want to hurt you. I want to *love* you."

"Oh!" Celia threw up her arms in exasperation. "Why does it have to be *love?* Why can't we just be the way we've been? Why don't we just kid around with each other, laugh and be happy together?"

"Sure, that's fun. But what about depth? What about really knowing one another? When I look at you, and our eyes meet, I feel a *connection* like nothing I've ever felt before!" Pained eyes stared into hers. "I have to believe that you feel it, too, or else I think I'd go crazy! But what good is that feeling if you're willing to walk right out of my life? What we have is rare. Some people never find it, but you're willing to throw it away." He sighed heavily. "And I've never felt so helpless in my life."

Celia struggled to hold back the tears. "Marcus, you're just asking too much. I can't give you what you want right now. I do care about you. I *do.* Please don't make it seem like I don't. It's just—"

"It doesn't matter, Celia. I'm not going to beg. Either you want to be with me or you don't. The decision is up to you." He shook his head.

His image became blurry as Celia stared at him through watery eyes. "Marcus, I need to do this show. It could be a big break for me."

"I realize that," he acknowledged solemnly.

"Part of me wants to stay…or at least come back. But I don't want to lead you on."

It took Marcus a full minute to respond. "Celia, once you leave, I'm going to need to get on with my life." His tone softened. "Not being with you is torture for me. I can't just keep on going the way we have been, waiting to see if your feelings change." He lowered his eyes. "If you don't love me, then please…don't come back."

"Are you saying…?" Celia faltered. "Once I'm gone, I'm gone?"

"More or less." He sounded so matter-of-fact.

"But I can't promise." She stumbled over her words. "Randy's show…you'll hate me if I go."

"Don't be silly," Marcus's voice was cold. "Who do you think sent Olmstead samples of your work?"

"What! You—?" Celia felt her world begin to spin.

"The photos from the burn site. I knew that if Randy saw them, he would be interested in your work."

"You sent them? Then…you don't mind if I go?" Her feelings of panic were so strong, Celia imagined they might actually be rising up to choke her. *It's too fast. This can't be happening.*

"How could I?" Marcus seemed on the verge of losing control of his emotions. "I can't tell you what to do. I have to let you follow your heart. Even if it's away from me."

"Marcus, you're making it sound like you don't matter to me. You *matter*—"

"Celia, don't." No amount of concentration could keep the anguish from his eyes. "I think it's best if you go," he said, his voice breaking.

238

"But can't we—," Celia drew in a sharp breath and moved as if in a daze toward the hallway. At the door she stopped and stared back at Marcus through red-rimmed eyes. "Not too long ago, somebody told me that I needed to start believing again. And I've tried. But it's just too hard to trust in what you're talking about…everlasting love." She wanted him to at least try to understand. "But there's one thing I have learned. There *are* good, loving people out there. You taught me that Marcus."

His voice was husky. "I'm glad to hear it. Good luck, Celia. I hope you'll be happy. I hope you stop hurting."

"At this moment," Celia whispered, "that's awfully hard to imagine."

Thirty

❧

"Remember me when I am gone away.
Gone far away into the silent land."
Christina Georgina Rossetti, 'Remember'

Heavy lids fell over tired, blue eyes. With a sigh, Marcus leaned back in his chair and concentrated on relaxing his shoulders as the strains of Tchaikovsky's *Dance of the Little Swans* filled the pine-scented room Eva had decorated for the holidays.

"Take a deep breath," Rob directed. "That's right. Now *relax*. Think good thoughts. *Good* thoughts."

Marcus opened one eye. "This is ridiculous. I feel like an idiot. You know, I can do this on my own."

"Right. That's why you've been putting it off all morning. Come on. Remember what the doctor said. You've got to calm down. You're a walking time bomb."

"*Was* a walking time bomb, thank you very much. That was three months ago."

"Don't bother me with details," Rob argued as he sat across from him.

"Don't you think you're going a little overboard? Nothing happened—"

"What do you mean, nothing happened? You about scared us to death with that little fit of yours! Eva about had an attack herself, driving you to the doctor."

"Rob—" A smile twitched at the corners of Marcus's mouth. "It was just *indigestion*."

His friend gave a heavy sigh. "Well, we didn't know that at the time. Besides, it was a sign from God."

"You're telling me my heartburn was from God?"

" 'Oh, ye of little faith.' Of *course* it was," Rob insisted. "If you hadn't had that bad spell when you did, you never would have gone in for a check-up, and you wouldn't have known that your blood pressure was up in the stratosphere. That's serious business, man. Do you want to have a *real* heart attack?"

"Stratosphere? Gee, it's nice to see that you aren't exaggerating the significance of the event," Marcus remarked dryly. "You know, Rob, lots of people have high blood pressure."

"Thank you, Dr. Kildare. Now start breathing."

"I really don't think these relaxation exercises are necessary."

"Doctor's orders. *Breathe.*"

Marcus folded muscular arms across his chest. "This isn't Lamaze, you know," he grumbled.

"All right, all right!" Rob finally relented. "You're on your own, then. I'll go see how Eva's doing. But if I catch you back on the phone in the next—," he glanced at his watch, "—forty-five minutes, you're in for another trip to the hospital. And this time, it won't be because of indigestion."

"I get the point." He watched as the designer strode across the room. "Hey, Rob?"

"Yeah?" Rob stopped at the door.

Marcus studied him thoughtfully. "Thanks. It's good to have you back."

Rob gave a careless shrug, as if the matter was never an issue. "No problem. After all, friends help friends. Isn't that right?"

"It is."

"Besides..." Rob laughed. "Every man's got his price. You made me an offer I couldn't refuse." Marcus watched as his friend moved into the hallway, closing the door behind him.

"I wish you weren't the only one." As was common during quiet moments, Marcus's thoughts turned to Celia. *Where is she now? What is her life like? Who is she with?*

It was tempting—*still* almost unbearably tempting—to call Randy and check up on her. But Marcus knew nothing good could come of such an action. She had made her decision. It was up to him to live with it.

His eyes grew damp as he reflected on the day she first appeared in his office rattled by the joke he and Rob had played, yet determined not to let her uncertainty show. *I don't know whether to die of embarrassment or ream you!* Fire had flashed in her eyes, making her look even more beautiful than she had on the evening they'd first met....

No!

Marcus shook his head, as if clearing away a mass of cobwebs. Such thoughts only tormented him. He reached across the desk for his pocket organizer; high blood pressure or not, he needed the solace of work. He needed something solid to occupy his mind. He needed....

The sound of voices in the hallway stopped him mid-reach.

"I'm breathing, I'm *breathing*," he said guiltily as the door flew open.

"Uh…I'm sure you are," Rob said uncertainly. Eva hung over his shoulder, looking worried.

"What's going on?"

Rob stretched out one hand in which he held a small piece of paper. "You got a telegram."

"What—?" Marcus stood.

His friend shrugged and handed the item to him, keeping wary eyes trained on his friend's face.

"Don't look at me like that!" Marcus said in an annoyed tone. "I'm sure I can handle it." But despite his brave words, his mind began to echo the old cliché: Telegrams always bring bad news.

He tore the paper open and began to read.

DEAR MARCUS STOP ALL IS WELL RANDY GREAT STOP I OWE ALL TO YOU STOP PLEASE COME TO SHOW DECEMBER 23 STOP CELIA STOP

"Everything okay?" Rob's concern was evident.

Marcus brushed a hand across his eyes. "Fine, fine." He handed Rob the telegram and sat back at his desk.

Rob read the message twice. "Marcus, that's next weekend."

"Yes, it is." Silence followed.

"Well?"

"Well, what?" The editor buried his head in his hands.

Rob let out his breath in exasperation. "Well, are you going to go?"

"I don't think so."

Eva moved from her position in the doorway and lay a hand on the younger man's shoulders. "But, Marcus, you love her."

"So?"

"So she needs you."

"No." His voice was crisp. "Celia Randall does not need me. If she did, she would have said so long ago. Maybe she misses me, but that's about it." Eva stared at him woefully as he pointed to the paper she now held. "Do you see anything in there about her wanting us to be together?"

"Well…no."

"Or loving me?"

"No, Marcus," Eva admitted.

"Well, then. Nothing's changed."

"But—," Rob tried one more time.

"End of discussion," Marcus barked. "I already have plans for the twenty-third, anyway. My folks and I are spending Christmas with relatives in the Midwest. I am not about to change my plans by opening up this can of worms again. I'm just starting to get my life back together, and I'd like to keep it that way.

"And now—" He eyed his hovering friends. "If you'll excuse me, I think I'm beginning to feel stressed out. I'd like to get back to Tchaikovsky."

Reluctantly, Rob and Eva turned toward the door.

"All right, but I just hope you're not making the biggest mistake of your life," Rob threw over his shoulder.

"So do I," Marcus stared at the closed door. "Believe me, so do I."

CHAPTER

Thirty-One

❦

"O that 'twere possible
After long grief and pain
To find the arms of my true love. Round once again!"
Alfred Lord Tennyson, *Maud*, II, 4

G ood morning, sunshine." Celia leaned over and scratched Hank's ears before pouring her coffee. "You're up awfully early. Are you excited, too?"

Hank wriggled happily, looking as if he was, indeed, eagerly anticipating the day's activities.

"Sorry, bub. But I can't take you with me today. We're going over final set-up at the studio. Look's like you'll have to stay at Dana's." She glanced out the window at the gray sky, then turned her eyes toward the neighboring yard, feeling thankful for gracious neighbors who were willing to provide "dog care." At just that moment, a dark-haired, bundled figure passed under the window, causing her to jump.

Could it be…? For months she had thought about Marcus, dreamed of being held in his arms once more. When she'd left Lundy, she'd wanted nothing more than to run to a place where there was no risk, no danger of getting hurt again. Her feelings for Marcus had been haunted by a fear so intense it had shaken her to the core. Only after months of longing, soul-searching, and timid efforts at prayer had she begun to realize that the only thing more terrifying was the prospect of living without him.

Her heart in her throat, Celia ran to the living room and threw the door open. *Oh, please, let it be him.* The sight of a man in uniform caught her up short.

"Telegram," he announced unnecessarily.

"Thank you." Celia's hand trembled as she signed. As the messenger walked back down the path, she retreated into the warm glow of her home and began to read:

DEAR CELIA STOP COULDN'T GET AWAY STOP GOOD LUCK YOU'LL BE GREAT STOP MARCUS P.S. FORGET WHAT I SAID BEFORE STOP NOT SORRY I MET YOU STOP

Celia lowered herself into the kitchen window seat, drew her knees up against her chest, and stared out through the glass, watching the dark clouds roll in. "Looks like I really blew it this time, Hank," she whispered. A slobbery muzzle nudged her hand. "I guess, despite everything, I thought he'd come."

Long-suppressed tears broke to the surface as she pulled her old friend into her arms. "Oh, Hank!" she mumbled against his fur. "I just wanted space. I didn't want him to stop *loving* me. And now that I finally know how I really feel, it's too late." Her slender shoulders shook in anguish. "God...please help me!"

"Flight number 328 to Chicago is now boarding at Gate Ten," a tinny voice announced. *"That's flight number 328 to Chicago. All*

passengers, please proceed to Gate Ten."

Marcus sighed and shifted a heavy, maroon garment bag to his left shoulder. "That's my flight," he muttered to no one in particular. *I hate traveling during the holidays.* He'd started his journey in the foulest of moods; after waiting nearly an hour to check his baggage, his patience was nearly spent.

"I can help the next person," called a tired voice from down the counter.

Marcus watched as the woman ahead of him approached the next available ticket agent.

"Come on, come on, hurry up" he urged under his breath. Dragging his fingers through his thick hair, he tried not to think about the message he'd sent. Surely, Celia had it by now. She'd know that he wasn't willing to be treated like a yo-yo. That he wasn't about to let her play with his emotions, play any games.

She's not playing a game. Regret had haunted him all day. As much as he hated to admit it, he knew the truth in his heart. Celia wasn't a game player. Eva was right. She had turned to him. And he had shut the door in her face.

"Final call. Flight number 328 to Chicago, boarding at Gate Ten."

Marcus stared at the speaker overhead and blinked at the announcement that followed.

"First call. Flight number 519 to Seattle, now boarding at Gate 13, please. That's flight number 519 at Gate 13."

"Next?"

He stepped forward and laid his ticket on the counter.

"Sir, you'll have to hurry. Your flight is now boarding."

Marcus shook his head impatiently. "Forget that. I need a

new ticket. You've got to get me on that flight to Seattle. I'll take First Class, if that's all that's available. I'll even fly cargo if I have to!" He leaned forward urgently. "But you've got to get me on that plane!"

"Good-bye, Randy!" the tiny brunette called from across the loft. "I'll see you later tonight, okay? Uh…Randy? Yoo-hoo!"

"What? Oh, sorry." The gallery owner kept his eyes trained on the piece before him. Thick fingers scratched at a black goatee streaked with white. "Hey, kiddo? Come over here, would you, and tell me what you think?"

"Not another one?" The woman smiled as she strode across the open, brick-walled room. "All right, all right. Let's see. What do I think…what do I think?" She linked her arm through his and thoughtfully considered the placement for a full minute before proclaiming, "I think it's absolutely perfect." She squeezed his hand affectionately. "Just like all the others. This show will be fantastic!"

"That's right," Randy Olmstead agreed proudly. "And you, my dear, are one of the main reasons why."

"Oh, stop it!" Celia's cheeks dimpled. "You're making me blush."

"That's all right. The color suits you." The thick-set man turned his full attention to the woman on his arm. "And so does that smile." He nodded his approval. "It's about time. I thought you were going to grouse about all day."

"I'm sorry, Randy," Celia apologized. "It's been a rough day."

"I know." He nodded. "He's not coming, is he?"

"How did you know?" Celia looked surprised. "Did he call you?"

249

"Oh, no. Not in the past four months. But I can picture him staying away. He's a good man, but a little proud." Randy patted her hand. "Well, there's no sense in beating yourself up over the whole thing."

"I know you're right, Randy." Celia sighed. "But it didn't have to be this way! I'm the one who messed everything up."

"Now, I won't listen to that kind of talk!" His voice was firm. "Love isn't about blame, you know. It's about growth."

"Maybe," Celia allowed. "If you're talking about growing *together.*"

"Well…not always. Sometimes love means giving the person you care about time. When you love someone, you need to consider what is in that person's best interest. This time has been good for you, Celia. You've really come a long way. Until today, you've been looking healthier. *Happier.* Much more at peace."

"I have been, Randy," she assured him. "It's just that these past few months, I've always pictured Marcus coming to the show, to see me. I can't believe it's really over."

"Huh. *I* can't believe you'd really let it be over."

Celia was confused. "What do you expect me to do?"

"Well, for goodness' sake, child! You've got two good feet, haven't you? You're the one who pushed the boy away. You can go after him!"

"But I don't think Marcus wants me anymore."

"Ha!" The man gave a derisive grunt. "I doubt that's true! Besides, you've hardly even given him a chance!"

Celia felt her heartbeat grow stronger.

"You really think that I should—?" she broke off, her eyes shining. "Randy, I think you're right! No, I *know* you're right. I'm going to go right home and pack...."

"Now, wait a minute! You're not going anywhere tonight, you know. Remember what I said about wanting what's best for people you care about? Well, I care about you, and there's no way I'm going to let my protégé take off on what could be the most important evening of her life." He ignored Celia's downcast look. "Show up on time tonight, say hello, do a little schmoozing... and then you can take off on your quest of the heart. Agreed?"

"Agreed."

"And, kiddo?"

"Yes?"

"Just don't forget that verse you keep quoting to yourself. No matter what happens with Marcus, you'll be all right."

Celia closed her eyes, remembering. "'For I know the plans I have for you,' declares the LORD. 'Plans to prosper you and not to harm you, plans to give you hope and a future.'" She smiled confidently and tugged at Randy's sleeve. "You're right. I've got hope and a future. And you're a part of it. Thanks for being such a great friend."

Randy put his arm around her shoulder and squeezed, like a benevolent uncle. "It's my pleasure, kiddo." Embarrassed by the show of emotion, he patted her hand one last time and then pushed her back toward the door. "Now, run along, and get yourself ready for tonight. Do I have to throw you out, for goodness' sake? What are you still doing here anyway?"

Celia rolled her eyes and grinned. "I can't *imagine...*"

Soft, golden candlelight illuminated the room, filled to overflowing with enthusiastic participants in culture and life, while outside, city lights twinkled in sync with the comfortable thump-

thump of the gathering's acoustic bass.

Randy cast a watchful eye on the man who sat fidgeting in the corner. Strikingly handsome in a stylish, black tuxedo, the tall man carried himself well and would have appeared at ease in the art crowd but for eyes that constantly searched the faces, and his nervous habit of running fingers through his hair, causing it to stand wildly on end. At one point, his eyes met Randy's, and a look of understanding passed between them.

After nearly forty-five minutes of wandering, Marcus moved to admire once more a particularly dramatic piece by Randy Olmstead's newest artist. This particular shot was a stark, black-and-white image, depicting the charred, lonely remains of what was at one time a living, majestic pine. Marcus studied it carefully, remembering the night Celia had mourned the loss of a dear friend.

Captured by the sound of melodious laughter, he turned and found himself face to face, once again, with the most beautiful woman he had ever laid eyes on.

Celia's face still seemed like that of an angel, her lips like roses, her eyes shining like stars. A beaded gown of emerald silk draped close, but not tightly, against her skin; slender calves and stylish black heels peeked out from beneath a fashionable, knee-length slit.

Drinking in the moment, Celia scanned the crowd with teary eyes, her face a mask of joy. Suddenly she turned her face back to one blurry yet familiar figure as all color drained from her cheeks.

"M—Marcus?"

Crossing the room with shaky steps, Celia struggled to maintain her composure. *I thought he...but I....* Then suddenly, gloriously, confusion gave way to pleasure, and she moved to join the man she loved. As she stood before him, smiling, despite the crowd of curious onlookers, Marcus reached out and pulled her into a warm embrace.

"Marcus," she whispered, her breath soft and gentle against his cheek. "What on earth are you doing here?"

His voice was urgent. "I had to come."

"But, Marcus, I thought you said you couldn't—"

"I was wrong, darling. Very wrong."

"We've been apart for so long. It's been four months—"

"—and three days."

"I was so afraid when you said you weren't coming!" Celia blinked away the tears. "I thought you hated me." She stared up at him, seeking any signs of forgiveness.

Marcus took her slender fingers and raised them to his lips. "I'd sooner despise the air I breathe."

Celia drew in a sharp breath, shaking her head in wonderment. "But...I still don't understand."

"Celia, it was a shock to hear from you. I had finally learned to deal with the emptiness, the feeling of loss." Marcus's eyes held hers, searching. "And then your telegram came. I wasn't sure what it meant. It was so unclear—"

"I thought you'd understand."

Marcus shook his head. "I couldn't hope." He squeezed her fingers gently, as if checking to make sure she really was there. "Darling, I'm so sorry about the way I pressured you. From the very beginning, you told me you weren't ready. But I just kept pushing. I couldn't accept it." He nodded solemnly and placed her hand over his heart. "Celia Randall, the day you left, it felt as if all the color had gone out of my life. I'm sorry I was impatient, that I thought only of myself. The last few months have been…unbearable. What you said is true, Celia. You're not a broken vase, and I can't solve all your problems. But when you face hard times, I want to be there with you. And from now on, when I'm dealing with difficulties, I want you with me, by my side." He gazed at her intently. "I don't want to waste another minute. I want us to be together for as long as God allows. I love you, Celia, with everything in me."

"Marcus! I don't know what to say! I—" Oblivious to the gathering crowd, including Randy's grinning face, Celia threw her arms around the man who haunted all her dreams, and the two pledged their love with an ardent kiss.

Finally roused by the sound of cheers, Marcus pulled away and cleared his throat, dropping to one knee. Ignoring the onlookers, he reached into his pocket and pulled out a tiny box covered with green velvet, bearing the name of a prominent Seattle jeweler. Celia's eyes grew wide as Marcus began, "Celia Randall—" Suddenly, he stopped and rose to his feet. "Wait a minute!"

"What? What!" Celia laughed at his theatrics.

"There's one more thing you should know. You may not want to hear another word from me once you find out what I've done with the magazine." He lowered his head, as if in shame.

"Oh, Marcus." Celia placed a gentle hand upon his sleeve. "Whatever it is, it'll be all right. I may not always agree with you, but I promise that no disagreement will ever keep me from loving you. We'll work it out together. I promise."

"Thank you." His voice was warm. "But I still think you should see this—" He reached inside his dress jacket and pulled forth a crumpled copy of *High Sierra*. "Look at the cover."

Hesitantly, Celia took the issue from his hand and scanned the article titles: "'Mono Revisited: A Progress Report,' 'Alkali Smog Alert,' 'Fowl Play: Hanging with the California Gull.' Hey, wait a minute!" She raised her eyebrows. "What is all this? Where's the fluff? What happened to the inns?"

"Oh, they're in there," Marcus assured her, tapping the cover. "Page 38. I wouldn't cut them completely. It meant too much to Charlie and Fee. But I'm afraid I did bump your piece way back. It's not even listed on the front. I figured you'd probably be pretty mad. So if you don't want to talk with me anymore, I understand—"

"Come here, you!" Celia threw her arms around Marcus's neck and showered his laughing face with kisses.

"Now, you realize this means I'm a potential failure, you Big Shot, you." He chuckled. "I spent the last four months trying to undo all the damage I'd already done. As a result, I may not be able to support you in the manner in which you are becoming accustomed."

"Oh, phooey!" Celia scoffed, fluttering her lips across his eyelids. "Who cares about that? You are a very good man, Marcus Stratton."

"I'm certainly glad you think so. Because if I have anything to say about it, you're going to be stuck with me for a *very* long time."

"Is that a promise or a threat?" She laughed.

"Oh, it's a promise." Marcus's voice became quite serious, then, and he dropped down again to one knee. "You better believe it's a promise." He slipped a hand into his pocket, drew out the jewelry box once more, and opened it before Celia's marveling eyes. "With this ring, I pledge you my heart and my life, my love and my devotion, my faithfulness and my faith, to be yours as long as we both shall live." Marcus's voice and hands shook. "To paraphrase the words of John Muir, 'whatever our fate, long life, short life, stormy or calm...because we are together, my love, we are rich forever.'" He raised the sparkling band to Celia's delicate finger. "I have little to give compared to all that you deserve. But everything I have—and am—is yours."

Marcus raised eyes brimming with love to her face. "Celia Randall, do you accept this ring and, with it, my heart?"

"Oh, I do!" Celia beamed with the joy of love worth the risk. "I do."

"This grand show is eternal.
It is always sunrise somewhere; the dew is never all dried at once;
a shower is forever falling; vapor is ever rising.
Eternal sunrise, eternal sunset, eternal dawn and gloaming,
on sea and continents and islands, each in its turn, as the round
earth rolls."

John Muir, *My First Summer in the Sierra*

About the Author

❧

Shari MacDonald is a full-time editor, writer and dog-lover from Portland, Oregon.

Sierra is Shari's first romance novel. Look for her second, in September 1995.

Dear Reader:

Although works of fiction are simply that—works of *fiction*—I cannot help but wonder if every author must put a bit of him- or herself into each story. I have to admit: *Sierra's* heroine and I are alike in more ways than one. We both sleep through the alarm, lose our keys—and I'm pretty sure Celia has bad hair days, too.

Not only that, I look forward to the day when I will have a "Hank" of my own. (For those of you who haven't read the book yet, please don't worry about me *too* much. Hank's the dog in the story, not the man.) As my parents would point out (and no doubt lament), I am, like Celia, a sentimental lover of canines: from Scamp, the stray mutt I cast as Toto in our fifth grade production of "The Wizard of Oz" (and who became one of my most loyal and loved friends for over fourteen years), to the beautiful but emotionally challenged Roxanne, whom I installed in my parents' household just months before moving out for the last time. (Dad pretended to grumble…but guess whose bed she sleeps on today? Hint: Not mine.)

More seriously, I, like Celia, have struggled with difficult spiritual issues: "Why doesn't God answer my prayers?" "Does God really love *me*?" And when faced with loss: "Why did God let this happen?" For years, I was afraid to admit I had questions and thought that I would be punished if the truth ever came out. Surely, other Christians would think that I was weak and evil? Most certainly, God would condemn me.

In time, however, I realized that the real sin was not in having questions about God, but in trying to hide those questions from him. I'm now much more honest with God in my search for truth. Meaningful answers don't always (or often) come easily. But I believe that faith becomes stronger once it's tempered by struggle. Real truth remains true under scrutiny. God is big enough for the tough questions. He's dealing with mine. He can handle yours, too.

I have no doubt.

Shari MacDonald
c/o Palisades
P.O. Box 1720
Sisters, Oregon 97759

Palisades...Pure Romance

Refuge, Lisa Tawn Bergren
Torchlight, Lisa Tawn Bergren
Treasure, Lisa Tawn Bergren
Secrets, Robin Jones Gunn
Sierra, Shari MacDonald
Westward, Amanda MacLean (April)
Glory, Marilyn Kok (April)
Love Song, Sharon Gillenwater (May)
Cherish, Constance Colson (May)
Betrayed, Lorena McCourtney (June)
Whispers, Robin Jones Gunn (June)
Angel Valley, Peggy Darty (July)
Homeward, Amanda MacLean (August)
The Garden, Shari MacDonald (August)
Hidden, Lisa Tawn Bergren (September)
Antiques, Sharon Gillenwater (September)
Echoes, Robin Jones Gunn (October)

Titles and dates are subject to change.

NOTE TO DEALER: Customer should provide 6 coupons and you should retain the coupon from the free book (#7). We will send you a replacement copy of the Palisades novel you give away via Spring Arbor, consolidated freight. (In Canada, contact Beacon Distributing.)

PLEASE FILL OUT:
(ON PAGE FROM FREE BOOK ONLY)

FREE BOOK TITLE _____

ISBN _____

STORE NAME _____

ADDRESS _____

_____

SPRING ARBOR CUSTOMER ID# _____
(VERY IMPORTANT!)

BEACON DISTRIBUTING ACCOUNT # (CANADIANS ONLY) _____

STAPLE THE 6 COUPONS TOGETHER WITH #7 AND THE INFORMATION ABOVE ON TOP.

YOU MAY REDEEM THE COUPONS BY SENDING THEM TO:

PALISADES CUSTOMER SERVICE
QUESTAR PUBLISHERS, INC.
P.O. BOX 1720
SISTERS, OR 97759

CANADIANS SEND TO:
BEACON DISTRIBUTING
P.O. BOX 98
PARIS, ONTARIO
N3L 3E5

BUY SIX GET ONE FREE — PALISADES FREQUENT BUYER COUPON

Applies to any Palisades novel priced at $8.99 and below.

Dealer must retain coupon from free Palisades novel.

Consumer must pay any applicable sales tax.

AT PARTICIPATING DEALERS